W9-AHO-586

Loving Lucy

DELPHI PUBLIC LIBRARY

222 East Main Street
Delphi, Indiana 46923
765-564-2929

Loving Lucy

An Illustrated Tribute To Lucille Ball

Bart Andrews and Thomas J. Watson

Foreword by Gale Gordon

Photographs from the Howard Frank Archives

St. Martin's Griffin
New York

For
Wanda Clark
and
Howard McClay
who love her, too
☆ ☆ ☆ ☆

Design by Paul Perlow

LOVING LUCY. Copyright © 1980 by Bart Andrews and Thomas J. Watson. All rights reserved. Printed in the United States of America. No part of this book may be used or reproduced in any manner whatsoever without written permission except in the case of brief quotations embodied in critical articles or reviews. For information, address St. Martin's Press, 175 Fifth Avenue, New York, N.Y. 10010.

Manufactured in the United States of America

Library of Congress Cataloging-in-Publication Data
Andrews, Bart.   Loving Lucy.

1. Ball, Lucille, 1911- 2. Entertainers—United States—
Biography. I. Watson, Thomas, 1948-   joint author. II. Title.

PN2287. B16A75 791.45'028'0924 [B]80-14152
ISBN 00-312-49975-2

FOREWORD ☆ ☆ ☆ ☆ ☆ ☆

To be asked to contribute an introduction to a biography of Lucille Ball is an honor that would flatter statesmen, inspire poets, and make innumerable superstars green with envy for not getting the assignment!

I am delighted to be the chosen one, but I have grave doubts about my ability to do the job. Introductions are tricky things. Some reveal too much, some too little. All too often they are lists of highlights from the subject's life, so voluminous and complete as to make reading the book unnecessary.

My concern increases when I realize that Lucille Ball is one of the few people in this world of whom it can truthfully be said, "Here is a lady who needs no introduction." That being the case, let me use the space allotted to me as a "thank you" note.

First, I have to thank the authors of this book for their graciousness in making room for my comments, and for including me in the body of this work. I am grateful to them for giving me the opportunity to sing the praises of a personality unique in our industry: a gifted comedienne, a brilliant technician, and a great lady. She is the only person I have ever met who deserves to be called a genius!

To You, Lucille, my heartfelt thanks for allowing me to work with you, to laugh with you, and, even on rare occasions, to cry with you. To share your joy when shows paid off, and to commiserate with you when you felt that the work at hand was less than perfect. Thank you for teaching me, by your example, that in our profession one's best is the very *least* we can do.

Mainly, dear heart, my thanks for letting me participate, in a very small way, in concocting the world's most needed tonic, laughter—the miracle drug! It's good for what ails you, it has no injurious aftereffects, and it is well nigh impossible to take an overdose!

The world loves you, dear physician. You have soothed our aches and pains, you have lightened our burdens and made our lives a little brighter, and you have given television an added dimension by using it as a vehicle for making house calls!

Bless you.

Gale Gordon

ACKNOWLEDGMENTS ☆ ☆ ☆ ☆ ☆ ☆ ☆

For their individual favors and cooperation, the authors wish to thank Marc DeLeon, Jr., Rick Carl, John Behrens, Bob Carroll, Jr., Madelyn Davis, Bill Chapman, and Jess Oppenheimer; the staffs at the libraries of the Academy of Motion Picture Arts and Sciences and the American Film Institute; the staffs of the Program Information Unit, CBS Broadcast Group and the Program Analysis Unit, NBC; the Howard Frank Archives for its unique collection of photographs (Box 50, Brooklyn, NY 11230); and the loyal members of We Love Lucy, the international Lucille Ball fan club (for membership information, send a self-addressed stamped envelope to P.O. Box 480216, Los Angeles, CA 90048).

CONTENTS ☆ ☆ ☆ ☆ ☆ ☆ ☆ ☆ ☆

1. Introducing Lucy	11
2. Lucy, the Showgirl	41
3. Lucy, the Starlet	59
4. Lucy, the Glamour Girl	93
5. Lucy, the Comedy Star	111
6. Everybody Loves Lucy	129
7. Starring Lucille Ball	163
8. The New Same Old Lucy Show Rides Again	179
9. Once More, Here's Lucy	201
10. Forever, Lucy	219
Index	225

★★★★★★ Introducing Lucy

She walked, she talked, she wiggled on her belly like a seal. She sang off-key, danced with two left feet, and conned her Cuban hubby into featuring her at his nightclub. Backfiring practical jokes left her handcuffed to her mate, glued to a white beard, and stuck with a loving cup on her head. She locked herself inside a deep-freeze, got drunk doing a TV commercial, and created her own, unique brand of chaos in New York, Los Angeles, Europe, Florida, Cuba, Connecticut, and points in between.

She insulted Ethel Merman to her face, locked her banker into a vault, and wore roller skates to a country club dance. She swam in a tank with a porpoise at Marineland and posed as a Hollywood stuntman. She got herself drafted, baby-sat a family of chimps, and ruined her employer's chances of being named "Boss of the Year."

She tried to teach her teenage son to drive and her daughter to shop for bargains. She broke into the Air Force Academy, rode the rapids of the Colorado River, learned to sky dive, then broke her leg skiing.

She assaulted, insulted, and badgered more than fifty celebrities, ranging from

Harpo to Tallulah to Richard Burton and Elizabeth Taylor.

She was a wife, a neighbor, the mother of one, a widow, the mother of two, the mother of none, a secretary, a sister-in-law. But above all else, she was a lady.

She dearly loved her husband and became overly jealous when another female came near. She waited up when her daughter went out on dates and went to work to buy her boy a bike. She bawled like a baby when her daughter announced she was leaving home.

She cared for her friends and neighbors and wept openly when it was time to move away. She lived in a bustling metropolis but fought to keep a small town on the map. She teased her brother-in-law about his dramatic talents but schemed to help him put on a show.

She was a Ricardo, a Carmichael, a Carter.

She was one part henna, one part illogic, three parts beauty.

She was love. She was "Lucy."

For well over a quarter of a century, beginning in 1951, gifted actress-comedienne Lucille Ball brought "Lucy" to life in over 500 individual performances, bringing laughter and mirth to television audiences the world over. And thanks to reruns, that laughter will never stop. *TV Guide* claims that Miss Ball has "a face seen by more people, more often, than the face of any human being who ever lived."

But it was not always so. As a teenager, Lucy spent four years pounding the pavement in New York, trying desperately to land a job on the stage. Her first break took her 3,000 miles away to Hollywood, where she spent another eighteen years fighting studio myopia and mediocre scripts. Only occasionally did she latch onto a property worthy of her talents.

During her Hollywood years, Lucy gladly did anything desired of her to stay in the public eye. When not working on a motion picture, she could be found modeling the latest fashions or endorsing the newest cosmetics in national magazine layouts. During the war, she joined the star-studded camp shows and helped sell Victory Bonds. She did charity work, radio programs, and toiled in two touring stage shows. But nothing—absolutely nothing—supplied the recognition and adulation she received from her work

in television.

Lucy's quest for stardom started in Celeron, New York, a village near Jamestown, where she was born on August 6, 1911. The daughter of Henry Dunnell and Desiree Hunt Ball, Lucy grew up with one great ambition—to be in show business. Every spring, it has been reported, she would run away and start walking south, in the direction of New York City, until someone inevitably found her and returned her home.

Much of the time, home was Grandpa's house. Shortly after Lucy's birth, Henry and Desiree (DeDe) moved to Butte, Montana,

where Ball worked as a telephone lineman. Three years later, he died of typhoid fever, and DeDe, pregnant with a second child, Freddie, returned to Celeron with young Lucy. The family found shelter with DeDe's parents, Fred C. and Florabelle Orchutt Hunt.

Grandpa was "a character," a man with an insatiable love of life who hated anything that tended to box a person in. His gift of love found its truest expression through activities with the children. He was always making things, and during the cold winter months he accompanied the children skating and sledding. In the summer, he planned picnics and boat rides. Weekends always brought shopping excursions and streetcar rides into nearby Jamestown, where he treated his wide-eyed brood to the visiting vaudeville show or to the movies. It was on these trips that Lucy was first exposed to the world of show busi-

15

ness. Tom Mix and Pearl White became her idols, and she knew immediately that someday she just *had* to become a part of their profession.

DeDe eventually remarried, to Edward Petersen, and the family moved to Jamestown. Although the marriage lasted only a year before DeDe filed for divorce, it was Petersen who first encouraged Lucy to pursue her dream. One evening Petersen took Lucy to see monologist Julius Tannen, who was appearing at the local high school. She was thrilled to see this man become different people just by changing his expression or altering his voice and posture. Lucy was hooked and before long was auditioning for every show business event in town. Every year she tried out for the Scottish Rite Revue and the Jamestown Players, appearing with the latter in *Within the Law.* High school plays became an obsession, and for one production, *Charley's Aunt,* she sold tickets, brought furniture from home to use as props, starred in a leading role, and helped clean the auditorium afterward.

Amateur plays, however, only whetted her taste for the real thing, and performing on the legitimate stage and in vaudeville became her secret wish. In 1927, at age fifteen, Lucy convinced DeDe that she was old enough to go to New York and study drama, where she enrolled in the John Murray Anderson School of Drama. What followed were the loneliest few months of her life. Desperately homesick, Lucy became a shy wallflower during class and impressed instructors as being too introverted ever to succeed in show business. The school's star pupil

was eighteen-year-old Bette Davis, who even at that early age could

☆ ☆ ☆ ☆ ☆ ☆

act up a storm. Her talent and assurance did nothing but scare the hell out of the reticent young girl from Jamestown.

Determined to prove her teachers wrong, Lucy left the school and landed a job in the chorus of the third road company of Ziegfeld's *Rio Rita*. After five weeks of rehearsal, she was fired. The director's opinion matched that of her instructors.

Hoping to alter her luck, Lucy changed her name to Diane Belmont. (She had always like the name "Diane," goddess of the hunt, and "Belmont" was borrowed from the New York racetrack.) Feeling that her background was as drab as her real name, she revised her résumé to reflect a hometown of Butte, Montana, where she had actually spent the first few years of her life. Butte, she reasoned, was more glamorous than tiny Celeron or Jamestown. To make her lie believable, she corresponded with every town in Montana big enough to have a chamber of commerce and memorized their handbills. She soon knew more trivia about the state than most Montanans.

Unfortunately, the new Western image did not help in the job market. Lucy joined the chorus of the Broadway musical, *Stepping Stones*, but the job lasted only a few weeks. A place in the chorus of *Step Lively* followed, but she was fired two weeks later. Disappointed, Lucy finally accepted everyone's advice and went home.

24

She returned to high school for a while but never graduated. By 1929 she was anxious to return to New York and give the town another whirl.

This time Lucy went not as a drama student, but as a working girl. She did part-time secretarial work during off-hours while answering producers' calls for show-girls during the day. Her first job on Broadway, however, was not in a show, but at a soda fountain. More part-time positions followed, but nothing compelling enough to make Lucy forget her dream. Unfortunately, the many positions did not pay more than a few cents an hour, and Lucy always seemed to be down to her last nickel. To survive, she subsisted largely on what she called "one donut guys," businessmen who ate at various Manhattan breakfast counters. She later explained, "They would order a cup of coffee and a couple of donuts, drink the coffee, eat one donut, leave their nickel for the counterman and go. I'd slide onto their stool, grab the nickel, and order my coffee and eat their donut."

While working as a soda jerk, Lucy studied modeling on the side. Soon Liggett and Myers hired her

to pose as "The Chesterfield Girl" in their cigarette billboard displays, and before long she became a model for dress designer Hattie Carnegie. The salary was only thirty-five dollars per week, but the Carnegie name carried prestige. She worked nights, posing for commercial photographers to earn extra money.

Carnegie hired models who looked like, or at least had similar measurements to, her most important customers. Lucy, one of her youngest showgirls, was chosen to model outfits for film stars Joan and Constance Bennett. To enhance the illusion, Lucy bleached her hair platinum blond and began combing it in the exact style worn by Joan.

One day, while modeling at Carnegie's showroom, Lucy was stricken with sharp pains shooting through her body. She collapsed and was taken to a local clinic. Ten days later, the illness was diagnosed as rheumatoid arthritis. The months of working odd hours and eating snacks instead of meals had finally caught up with her. Lucy was now suffering from severe malnutrition and physical exhaustion.

She returned to her mother's home in Jamestown where she was bedridden for over two years. The arthritis had damaged the muscles in her legs, and she literally had to learn to walk all over again. Once

on her feet, however, she and a new girl friend started talking about New York. Lucy was anxious to return to the city, and a few weeks later, in the spring of 1933, the two boarded a bus.

Lucy got her job back with Hattie Carnegie and later joined Mrs. E. A. Jackson, a former Carnegie employee who had resigned to go into business for herself. Then, one hot afternoon in July, Lucy ran into Sylvia Hahlo, an actors' agent who was coming out of an office above the Palace Theatre.

"How would you like to go to California?" Sylvia asked an excited Lucy. "I just came from Sam Goldwyn's office, and they have had one of their showgirls back out. They have to leave for Hollywood on Saturday, and they need another girl."

The picture, Lucy learned, was to be an Eddie Cantor musical, *Roman Scandals,* and the producer wanted all of the chorus girls to have had exposure as poster girls. Because of Lucy's tie-in with Chesterfields, she fit the bill.

Three days later, with heart in hand, Lucy boarded a train for Hollywood. The movie, she figured, would keep her busy at least six weeks, and, if nothing further developed, she could always return to New York and continue modeling.

★ ★ ★ ★ ★ ★

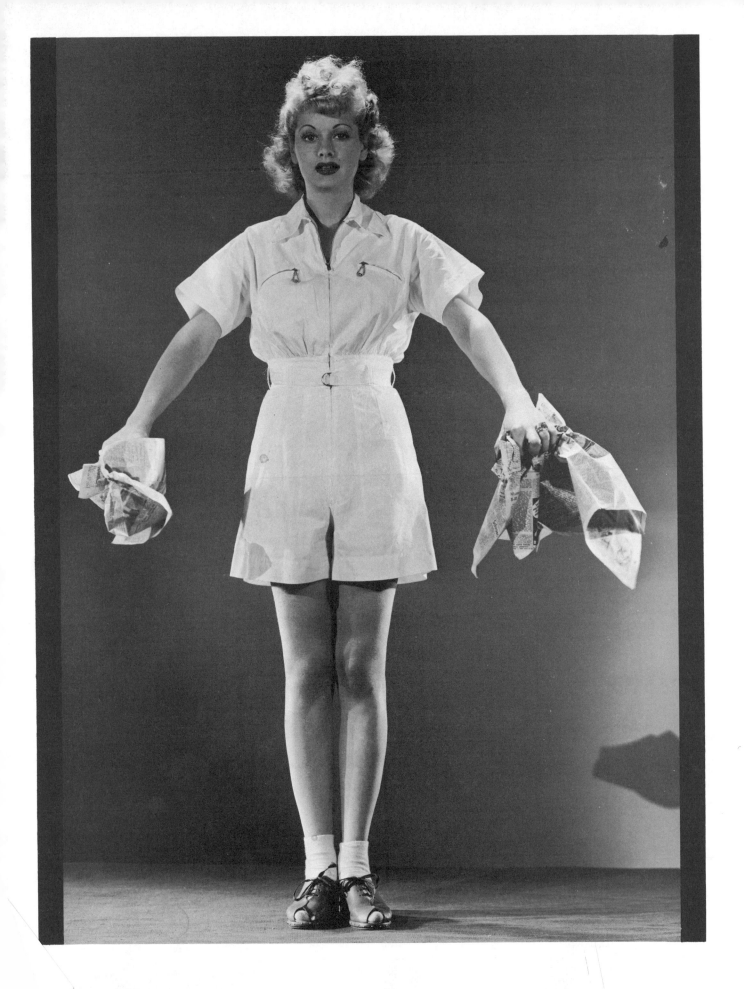

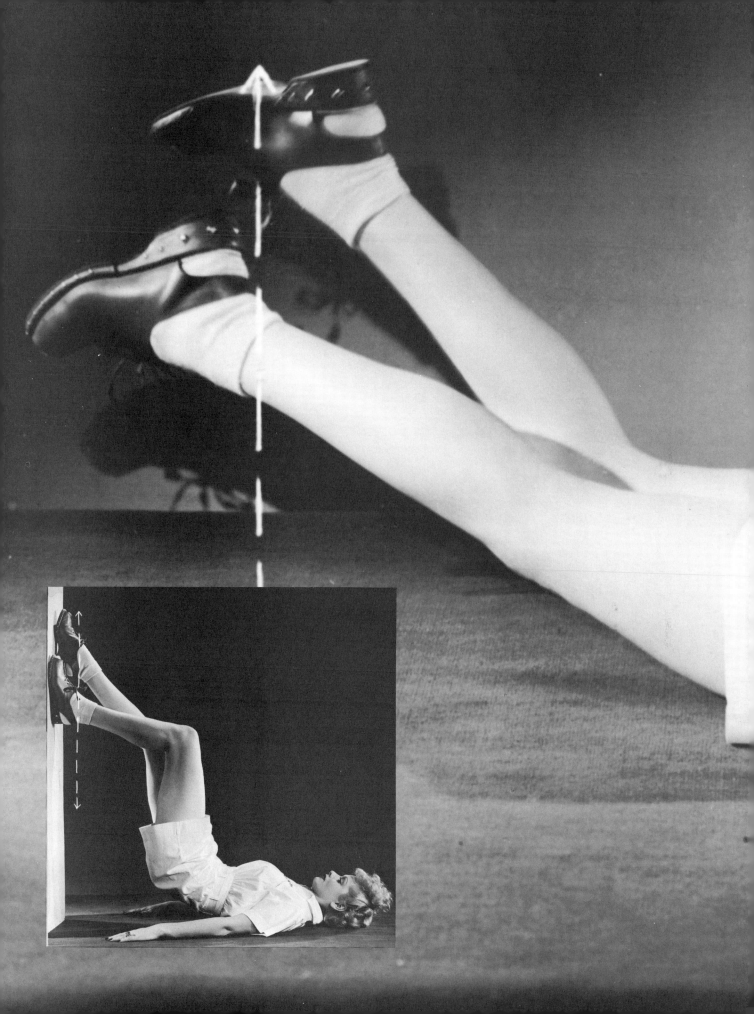

Hollywood Hopefuls: Seven beautiful poster girls arrive from New York July 19, 1933, to begin work as Goldwyn Girls. Right to left: Katherine Mauk, Rosalie Fromson, Mary Lange, Vivian Keefer, Barbara Pepper, Theo Phane, and Lucille Ball.

Roman slave girl Lucille Ball (left) in a scene with Eddie Cantor from *Roman Scandals*.

★★★★★ Lucy, The Showgirl

Twenty-two-year-old Lucy (front row, second from left) adds a touch of glamour to *Bottoms Up,* a 1934 Fox film starring Spencer Tracy.

*T*hey came from everywhere: north, south, east, and west. They were young; they were tall. Some were blond, some brunette, some redheaded. But most of all, they were beautiful. They were the Goldwyn Girls, Hollywood's answer to Broadway's glorification of the American female, the Ziegfeld Girl.

Producer Samuel Goldwyn started the tradition in 1929, when casting commenced on the Eddie Cantor musical, *Whoopee.* A Cantor film extravaganza was created every year thereafter, and with it came a new bevy of Goldwyn beauties. By July 1933, the Goldwyn staff, with a major assist from Busby Berkeley, had chosen its fourth annual roster of glamorous showgirls, this time for Cantor's *Roman Scandals,* and, according to a *Hollywood Reporter* article, the selection process had taken an interminable nine months. More than 8,000 applicants had been screened, and one of the final positions, it was noted in the newspaper, "went to the girl whose smiling face adorned the Chesterfield cigarette billposters."

Lucille Ball, still blond from her Hattie Carnegie modeling days, arrived in Hollywood in mid-summer and began what ultimately would be a one-year apprenticeship with Goldwyn, at a salary of $150 a week. Rehearsals for *Roman*

Lucille Ball, *Kid Millions*, 1934.

Lucy's tenth screen appearance, and her last for producer Sam Goldwyn, is in *Kid Millions.* (She is the blonde behind Eddie Cantor's right shoulder.)

★ ★

Scandals started almost immediately, but because both Cantor and Goldwyn were perfectionists, more than three months elapsed before the film was actually completed. In the meantime, Lucy had done walk-ons in two features (*Broadway Thru a Keyhole* and *Blood Money*) produced by Darryl F. Zanuck under his new 20th Century Productions banner. Since Zanuck and Goldwyn both released their product through United Artists—and to help get 20th rolling—Goldwyn loaned Zanuck various personnel, including a few of his contract players.

Lucy also made a brief appearance in *Nana,* a screen adaptation of the Émile Zola novel, starring Anna Sten, which Goldwyn was shooting simultaneously with *Scandals.* Bit parts in two films for the Fox Corporation and three more for 20th Century followed (the two companies had not yet merged), but Lucy began to fear she might never progress beyond the showgirl stage.

Basically still shy and reticent, twenty-two-year-old Lucy nevertheless took to wearing a somewhat brassy veneer around the Goldwyn lot in hopes of being noticed. She literally cajoled screenwriter Arthur Sheekman into giving her a line of dialogue—her first—in *Roman Scandals* and

soon became the "class clown" on the set. Goldwyn himself fell victim to her playful shenanigans as she campaigned for bigger and better roles. Sam, however, was an independent producer, averaging two or three pictures a year. The best he could offer the ambitious Miss Ball in 1934 was a continuation of her chorus line duties, this time in Eddie Cantor's fifth film musical, *Kid Millions.*

George Murphy, Ann Sothern, and Ethel Merman co-starred in that one, and in his memoirs, Murphy recalled that Lucy tried everything to resist being labeled "last year's showgirl." During the shooting of the musical numbers,

Clowning on the set of *Three Little Pigskins*, a Three Stooges short, Lucille scored as a member of Columbia Pictures' new stock company.

assistant director Ben Silvie would give the company periodic five-minute breaks. Invariably, Lucille would be late in returning, and Silvie would have to call her name over the loudspeaker. When Murphy asked Lucy why she was "misbehaving," she replied that although she knew she could be fired, at least "they'll know who I am!"

In August 1934, Lucy took a chance and left the Goldwyn den to become a contract player at Columbia Pictures, taking a salary cut to seventy-five dollars per week. Columbia was one of the smaller studios at the time, but it offered Lucy a chance to work in comedy, which she already felt would be her forte. She became

part of Columbia's resident "stock company" of young players and scored in a few two-reel comedy shorts, including *Three Little Pigskins* starring the irrepressible Three Stooges, and *Perfectly Mismated* with Leon Erroll. However, the five features in which she was assigned bit parts, oddly enough, were straight dramas. In the first four—*Broadway Bill, Jealousy, Men of the Night,* and *Fugitive Lady*—Lucy appeared without billing. *Carnival,* her fifth flick for the studio, supplied her first on-screen credit, for a small role as a nurse. Ironically, by the time the picture opened February 15, 1935, Lucy had started work elsewhere.

The move had occurred on November 26, 1934, when Columbia abruptly decided to cut costs by dissolving its company of contract players. Lucy was despondent, having just invited her family to move west from New York. A friend saved the day by pointing out that RKO Pictures—located just down Gower Street from Columbia—was holding a casting call *that very*

night for showgirls for the new Irene Dunne-Astaire-Rogers musical, *Roberta.* Lucy dashed to the audition, landed the job, and was destined to remain at RKO for seven years. The new assignment boasted the meager salary of fifty dollars per week, but for Lucy it was the *doing* that was most important. Years later, she would look back on the couple of hours that had elapsed between her Columbia and RKO engagements as the only time she was ever unemployed in Hollywood, surely some sort of record in a town noted for chronic employment instability.

RKO, an entertainment conglomerate with roots in radio and vaudeville, had, by 1935, suffered the worst blows that the Depression had to offer and was fighting its way out of bankruptcy with a string of consistently fine, medium-budget films. Katharine Hepburn and Irene Dunne headed the studio's roster of stars, a list that also included Ginger Rogers, Fred Astaire, Ann Harding, Anne Shirley, and Richard Dix. Lela Emo-

Autumn 1934. Lucille Ball waits for Columbia to assign her a decent part.

A. Lucy on the town with Mack Grey, George Raft's right-hand—er, make that left-hand—man. Raft had befriended Lucy during her early Goldwyn days and, in late 1934 when this photo was taken, loaned her rent money and the use of his limousine to pick up her arriving family at the train station.

B. A homemaker at heart, Lucy moved her mother, brother, grandfather, and cousin into her new bungalow at 1344 North Ogden Drive in West Hollywood.

C. Happy New Year and goodbye: Lucy (far right) and fellow Columbia contract players were pink-slipped shortly after posing for this year-end publicity shot.

1935

R-PUB-T
P-803-7

gen Rogers, Ginger's "backstage mama," headed the studio's New Talent School and was responsible for training and nurturing the studio's up-and-coming unknowns.

Lucille Ball was still about as unknown, at least by the general public, as any aspiring actress could be in 1935, a situation that long hours of study with Mrs. Rogers would soon correct. Lucy's brief but stunning appearance as a fashion model in *Roberta* prompted RKO executives to give her a contract, and recommendations from Lela and Ginger led to parts in three new features. The roles were small, but Lucy was learning her craft, taking things one step at a time, and working with some of the finest talent in Hollywood. *Old Man Rhythm,* in which Lucy played a campus coed, starred Charles "Buddy" Rogers; *Top Hat,* of course, headlined Rogers and Astaire; and *I Dream Too Much* starred Henry Fonda and Lily Pons. All were musicals: Hermes Pan choreographed the first two, and Pandro S. Berman produced the latter pair.

Over her better judgment, Lucy completed the year by making an unbilled appearance as an "extra" in *The Three Musketeers,* with Walter Abel, and joined the entire stable of RKO contract players, including her new buddy Betty Grable, in a two-reel short, *A Night at the Biltmore Bowl.* Lucy later recalled these early years: "I talked

A. One of a dozen, Lucy (fourth from bottom) poses with her fellow *Roberta* models.

B. A facsimile of Lela Rogers' performance record card for Lucille Ball, 1935–37.

A Parisian fashion show, in which Lucy models a gown of ostrich feathers, climaxed RKO's *Roberta.* The clothes, designed by Bernard Newman, cost $250,000—one-third of the film's entire budget.

to everyone I met, from office boys to executives—possibly because of that urgent need I'd always had to make people like me—and I posed for every cheesecake picture they asked for. I could never say no."

For Lucy, 1936 was what sports fans call a "building year," a period of gradual but perceptual professional growth. The parts were slowly but surely getting bigger, and Lucy was winning the attention of the front office. Her assignments included five features, most memorable of which was *Follow*

the Fleet, starring Astaire and Rogers, Randolph Scott, and—making her motion picture debut—Harriet Hilliard. (Betty Grable was also in the cast.) In one scene, as Lucy and some other showgirls arrive on deck of a schooner to rehearse a benefit show, they are ogled by love-starved but bashful

B

C

D

sailors. One particularly burly seaman approaches Lucy with "How was heaven when you left?" Lucille deadpans: "Tell me, little boy, did you get a whistle or a baseball bat with that suit?"

Lucy also performed in such comedy two-reelers as *So and Sew,* with Anne Shirley, and *One Live Ghost,* with Leon Errol.

Close chum Barbara Pepper, a fellow New Yorker and ex-Goldwyn Girl, joined Lucy in RKO's ambitious production of Maxwell Anderson's *Winterset,* but Betty Grable, tiring of small parts, went across the street and signed on with Paramount. Lucy continued to make friends on the lot and later admitted, "I've always been a family person, and I adopted RKO as my studio family."

In August 1936, her studio "parents" agreed to loan Lucy to playwright Bartlett Cormack for his Broadway-bound production of *Hey Diddle Diddle,* but then postponed the offer when a part became available for her in the new Lily Pons film, *That Girl from Paris.* The decision was a wise one, for the picture brought Lucy her first bankable reviews. The *New York Daily Mirror* called her "an able actress and an agile dancer," whose scenes were "worth the whole price of admission." The review concluded that she "rates . . . more conspicuous roles and more intense promotion. She is a comedienne, which is always a 'find.'"

A. Being groomed for RKO stardom, in February 1936, were (left to right) Lucille Ball, Margaret Callahan, Joy Hodges, Anne Shirley, Phyllis Brooks, and Molly Lamont. Lucy, Joy, and Phyllis appeared in *Follow the Fleet,* released later that month.

B. Designer Bernie Newman congratulates Lucy (left), Jane Hamilton, and Kay Sutton, who were just awarded RKO contracts, March 25, 1935.

C. *Top Hat,* in which Lucy appears briefly as a florist's clerk, afforded her only one line of screen dialogue—but bigger parts were on the way.

D. Current fashion layouts kept performers in the public eye. Lucy is pictured here, *circa* November 1935, while appearing as Gwendolyn Dilley in *I Dream Too Much,* a Jerome Kern musical.

F. Lucy (right) and her friend Jane Hamilton appeared together as college coeds in RKO's *Old Man Rhythm.*

NY-1Z-

Lucille Ball, age twenty-four.

A. Modeling for publicity, Lucy sports a 1936 white sharkskin suit styled with a tailored collar and three patch pockets.

B. Lucille Ball, *Follow the Fleet*, 1936.

"Best-Dressed Girl in Town": Lucy won the title in June 1936, the
first time Hollywood stylists did not bestow the honor on an established star.

52

Follow the Fleet starred Fred Astaire and Ginger Rogers as—what else?—a song-and-dance team. Lucy played one of Ginger's friends.

Relaxing on the set of *Follow the Fleet*, Ginger, Lucy, and Harriet scan fan magazine clippings for the latest town gossip.

So and Sew, an RKO two-reel short, starred (left to right) Anne Shirley, Lucille Ball, and Patricia Wilder.

Lucy and Betty Grable make dowdy Harriet Hilliard more glamorous to help her catch a man in *Follow the Fleet*. The girls, off the screen, remained lifelong friends.

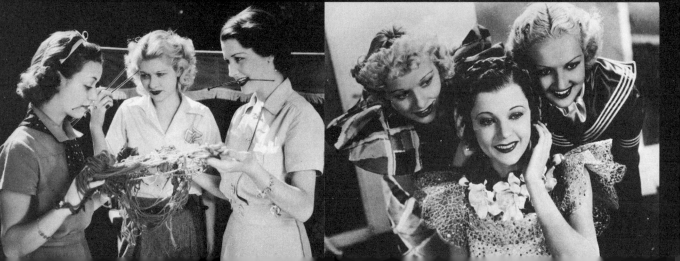

Disappointment does not show as Lucy returns to California and RKO, after a two-month road tour in Bartlett Cormack's *Hey Diddle Diddle.*

Lucy's platinum locks were darkened to a more natural honey-blond for her role in *Bunker Bean,* a 1936 comedy.

Designer Bernard Newman, later affiliated with Bergdorf Goodman, escorts Lucy for an evening at the Trocadero, a popular Hollywood night spot.

An appearance in a rather routine Guy Kibbee-Una Merkel comedy, *Don't Tell the Wife*, followed, and it was Christmastime before Lucy finally boarded a train bound for the East and *Hey Diddle Diddle*. The comedy, starring Conway Tearle, a matinee idol of the silent era, premiered at the McCarter Theatre in Princeton, New Jersey, on January 21, 1937, moved on to Philadelphia and Washington, D.C., but closed on February 13 when Tearle, age fifty-nine, suddenly became gravely ill. Lucy managed, however, to pick up an excellent notice in *Variety:* "[She] fattens a fat part and almost walks off with the play. She outlines a consistent character and consistently gives it logical substance. Has a sense of timing, and, with few exceptions, keeps her comedy under control."

The review did not go unnoticed at RKO. Returning to California, Lucy was greeted by an excited Lela and Ginger Rogers who had found what they considered to be the perfect showcase for Lucy's emerging talents—the role of the wisecracking Judith Canfield in the upcoming screen version of the Kaufman-Ferber hit, *Stage Door*.

Lucy's days as a minor showgirl were clearly behind her.

Football collegiate all-stars, at RKO to appear in a 1936 film, *The Big Game,* pose with the studio's top starlets. (Front row, left to right) Patricia Wilder, Barbara Pepper, Lucille Ball, and (back row) Anne Shirley.

RKO dance director, Hermes Pan, Fred
Astaire's choreographer-partner, coached
Lucy for her dance routines in the Lily Pons
musical, *That Girl from Paris.*

A touch of sable highlighted
Lucy's gray wool outfit,
modeled here in late 1936,
prior to her trip East.

L·B·318

★★★★★★★ Lucy, The Starlet

Ladies of the Theatre: Kate, Lucy, and Ginger portray girls waiting for their first big break on the Broadway stage.

Webster's Dictionary defines a starlet as "a young movie actress being coached and publicized for starring roles." Such was the case as Lucille Ball progressed from the "showgirl" to the "starlet" stage of her budding film career. However, it happened almost in spite of, rather than because of, the fabled Hollywood star system. This was not so much the fault of the system itself, as of Lucy's current benefactor, RKO. To function properly, the star system required continuous, careful, and steady supervision. The only thing continuous at RKO in the late thirties was chaos.

Film historian and director of the cinema collection at the Los Angeles County Museum of Art, Ron Haver, explains: "Of the major studios, RKO was the only one that did not have people with long experience and knowledge of film at the corporate level. The others had been founded and developed by individuals who cared passionately about films. . . . They took pride in their work, and the boards of directors of their corporations were wise enough to leave them alone to make pictures . . . which is exactly what the RKO board of directors seldom, if ever, did. . . . Shifts in management often involved complete change of policy. . . .

Lucille Ball, 1941.

Because of the constant pulling, tugging, and bickering at the top, there was a lack of long-range planning. Little attention was paid to what went on at the studio, except to bring in a new production head every several years. . . ."

If the overall studio product also lacked continuity of quality and style, it was no wonder that the pictures assigned to various contract players, including Lucille Ball, were so eclectic. Only the established superstars of the day, people like Katharine Hepburn, could pick and choose their own material.

RKO's "big show" in 1937,

Ginger and Lucy prepare for a night out on the town with two visiting lumberjacks—anything for a decent meal.

Residents of the Footlights Club.

Stage Door, had been acquired for $130,000 by producer Pandro S. Berman as a vehicle for the afore-mentioned Hepburn, who had recently suffered the indignity of having three successive films bomb at the box office. Taking no chances with *Stage Door,* Kate spent the winter of 1936–37 work-

ing closely with Berman, director Gregory LaCava, and scriptwriters Morrie Ryskind and Anthony Veiller, making subtle changes in the screenplay.

The plot centered around the young residents of the fictional Footlights Club, a Manhattan haven for aspiring actresses, mod-

Ann Miller, a fourteen- (yes, fourteen!) year-old hoofer Lucy spotted in San Francisco, received her big break when Miss Ball convinced RKO to cast her as Ginger Rogers' dancing partner in *Stage Door.*

eled closely after the real life Rehearsal Club. Berman planned to team Hepburn with the studio's rising young musical comedy star, Ginger Rogers. Hepburn would play a wealthy debutante idealist, while Ginger, in a change of pace role, would be cast as the flip, almost cynical pragmatist, Jean Maitland.

had made recently for Universal and hired her as another of the Footlights Club stagestruck hopefuls.

Andrea Leeds, who played a suicide victim in the film, later recalled LaCava's effective direction: "He had all us girls in the movie come to the studio for two weeks before the shooting started and

was an immediate success for everyone involved. As a result, RKO rewarded Lucy by revising her contract, providing for periodic salary increases.

Unfortunately, no quality film like *Stage Door* was on the studio drawing boards that fall. A lackluster comedy, *Joy of Living*, was already in the can awaiting re-

Camp Kare-Free is the setting for *Having Wonderful Time*, a Ginger Rogers vehicle. Featured here are Lucy and Lee Bowman.

Joy of Living was originally titled *Joy of Loving*, but the Hays Office blue-penciled it on the theory that there should be no "joy" in "loving."

Ginger and mama Lela recognized *Stage Door* to be one of the prestige films of the year and convinced producer Berman that Lucy would be just right for one of the supporting roles, Judy Canfield (played on the New York stage by Lee Patrick). Director LaCava remembered a screen test that twenty-four-year-old Eve Arden

live as though we were in the lodging house itself. He had a script girl take down our conversations and he would adapt these into dialogue. He rewrote scenes from day to day to get the feeling of a bunch of girls together—as spontaneous as possible."

Stage Door opened October 7, 1937, at Radio City Music Hall and

lease, but Lucy was not very enthusiastic about her role as Irene Dunne's selfish kid sister. Moreover, Lela Rogers was preparing to spend the better part of the coming year in New York working on a play; both Lucy and Ginger would be deprived of her valued guidance.

Lela's two protégées again

teamed up for *Having Wonderful Time,* a routine comedy set at a Catskills resort hotel. Again Lucy's part was unsympathetic—that of star Ginger's roommate—but it did provide for many scenes with newcomer Richard "Red" Skelton, making his motion picture debut. (Eve Arden was also in the cast.)

who also starred in a few movies, heard Lucy on the Baker broadcast and requested that RKO cast her as his wife in the film, *Go Chase Yourself.* The feature was described by one critic as a "guileless slapstick comedy geared for the family trade," but *Variety* pointed out that "Miss Ball does excellently in a somewhat repressed

later put it, "a kind of second-rate star." She portrayed Annabel Allison, a fading but temperamental film star whom Oakie, as studio publicist Lanny Morgan, tries to keep in the public eye via various mad schemes. *Annabel* was a hit—*Variety* concluded that her casting had been justified "by a good performance"—and RKO planned

Joe Penner, famous for his one-liner, "Wanna buy a duck?", sold RKO on casting Lucy in *Go Chase Yourself,* 1938.

Phil Baker, popular radio comedian, with Lucy, 1937.

On November 7, 1937, Lucy became a regular on *The Phil Baker Show,* a comedy-variety series heard weekly over CBS Radio. A former vaudevillian, Baker had started in radio a few years earlier, and his half hour of music and gags had, by 1937, become one of the nation's Top Ten favorites.

Joe Penner, a fellow radio comic

role," and the *New York Journal American* called her "one gorgeous eyeful."

RKO was sufficiently pleased by Lucy's comedic bent to give her the female lead in Jack Oakie's new movie, *The Menial Star.* Ultimately retitled *The Affairs of Annabel,* the film established Lucille Ball as both a redhead and, as she

to issue a series of sequels. The first, *Annabel Takes a Tour,* was rushed into production that same year, but it lacked the sparkle of the original. Plans for yet another sequel fell through when Oakie and RKO disagreed over salary.

Nevertheless, Lucy's work schedule was far from empty. RKO had just purchased screen rights

Cover girl-actress Annabel Allison provided Lucy with her first successful starring role.

to George Abbott's Broadway comedy, *Room Service*. The Marx Brothers were borrowed from MGM (having just completed *A Day at the Races*), and Lucy and Ann Miller were set to co-star. The

★ ★ ★ ★

her own. She's always needed a script."

Garson Kanin, fresh from Broadway and a short apprentice-

★ ★ ★ ★

The Affairs of Annabel, teaming Lucy with Jack Oakie, was written by Bert Granet, later an exec producer for Desilu Productions.

finished product turned out to be a major disappointment: Because the original Broadway script was followed to the letter, the brothers Marx were allowed no ad-libbing, Lucy no mugging, and Ann Miller no dancing. Obviously, no one—including film audiences—was satisfied.

Groucho, in later years, did not recall noticing signs of Lucy's later comic "genius" during the five weeks that *Room Service* was in production. "She's an actress, not a comedienne," he said. "There's a difference. I've never found Lucille Ball to be funny on

ship with Sam Goldwyn, signed with RKO in 1938 and was chosen to direct Lucy in her next film, the first for which she would receive top billing. Kanin recalls: "I had made one small film called *A Man to Remember*. I was immediately assigned to a run-of-the-mill nonsense, objected, was told to do it or else, chose to do it, and suffered through it."

The same can be said of Lucy. The "nonsense," titled *Next Time I Marry*, concerned a spoiled heiress who is forced to marry an American citizen—*any* American citizen—in order to collect her inheritance. She rapidly exchanges vows with a ditchdigger, planning all along to dump the sucker in a

Lucille Ball, *Annabel Takes a Tour*, 1938.

The White Way Hotel still has not recuperated since Lucy and the Marx Brothers first rang for *Room Service*.

★★ ★★★★★★

quickie Reno divorce. She discovers—at the last possible moment, of course—that she really cares for the guy, and love conquers all. As *Variety* concluded, "Miss Ball deserves better. Story is banal, production values poor, direction sloppy.... Only Lucille Ball's and James Ellison's terrific struggle with bad material saves the production from being much worse."

Lucy and virtually every other actress in Hollywood that autumn (1938) checked in at David O. Selznick's Culver City studio to test for the part of Scarlett O'Hara in *Gone With the Wind*, the most sought-after role in film history. Of course, Lucy did not get the role—but some twenty years later she wound up buying the entire Selznick lot!

A flurry of RKO acting assignments—four dramas, three comedies—followed the *Wind* screen test, all of them so-called "B" pictures. Few, if any, served to advance or enhance Lucy's career. *Beauty For the Asking*, for example, featured her as a beauty-shop operator who wins in business but loses at love. *Variety* again scolded the studio, repeating the plea, "Lucille Ball . . . deserves much better material than she has been getting.... She is one of the more promising young players on the RKO contract list."

After the studio's plans to re-team Lucy with Joe Penner in a new comedy failed to materialize, they co-starred her instead with Richard Dix in *Twelve Crowded Hours*, a routine melodrama. One reviewer considered Lucy "fairly effective" in her role of a crime reporter's girl friend, while a second lamented, "Miss Ball plays it with just the appropriate air of somnambulism."

Even worse was *Panama Lady*, one of RKO's all-time losers. Lucy played a stranded nightclub entertainer who tries to rehabilitate an alcoholic geologist. The film received universally poor reviews when it was released in June 1939 and has recently been described as "the nadir" of Lucy's B-picture period.

Author Nathaniel West, who had just published his searing novel about Hollywood, *The Day of the Locust*, joined RKO in 1939 and was assigned to write screenplays for the B unit. The first of these was *Five Came Back*, to be co-authored with Jerry Cady and Dalton Trumbo. West knew that in order to receive solo credit on future films, his early collaborative efforts would have to be hits. *Five Came Back* was just that. A precursor of the "disaster" films of the seventies, *Five Came Back* told a highly effective and gripping story about an ill-fated airliner that crashes in the Brazilian jungle with twelve passengers aboard. There is a struggle against time—and a gaggle of nearby headhunters—to get the crippled craft into condition to fly again. Once the plane is repaired, it will bear the weight of only five passengers: How will the lucky five be chosen?

Chester Morris starred in the ★ film as the pilot, but Lucy had second billing as one of the passengers, a wayward girl with the proverbial heart of gold. *Five Came Back* opened on the fourth of July, 1939, to unexpectedly fine reviews. One columnist summed it up as "a tight, exciting little picture. . . . This is what the movie business calls a 'sleeper.' In other words, an unheralded, fairly inexpensive little picture with an unexpected punch."

RKO interrupted Lucy's string of melodramas with a lightweight musical, *That's Right, You're Wrong*, a showcase for Kay Kyser and his orchestra. Lucille Ball, Dennis O'Keefe, and Adolphe Menjou headlined the cast, which also included such favorite character actors as Edward Everett Horton, Roscoe Karns, May Robson, Moroni Olsen, and Horace McMahon. Hollywood gossip columnists Hedda Hopper and Sheilah Graham portrayed themselves. The plot, thin as it was, concerned a popular bandleader who goes to Hollywood to make a movie, only to have the project fall apart when the studio's top writers cannot dream up the right story. The proceedings were all in fun and reminded audiences of Lucy's skill at comedy.

The Marines Fly High, Lucy's first film in 1940, reunited her with former co-stars Richard Dix and Chester Morris in yet another stale melodrama set in Central America. (Europe, by this time, was at war and no longer seemed the appropriate setting for Hollywood escapist entertainment.) Lucy played the proprietress of a cocoa plantation who joins forces with marines Dix and Morris in a struggle with local *banditos*. Critics blasted the film with such adjectives as "trite," "implausible," "silly," and "inane." *Variety*, however, continued to give Lucy the benefit of the doubt, noting "she again demonstrates she is an up and coming young actress."

The problem, of course, was that Lucy's career had been idling in this neutral "up and coming" status for almost five years. She yearned for the kind of Class-A roles friends Ginger Rogers and Carole Lombard (who had joined RKO in 1939) were getting. *You Can't Fool Your Wife*, another nonsensical domestic comedy, only frustrated her further.

But finally, in April 1940, Lucy was offered a plum part in *Dance, Girl, Dance*, which had promise of being her best assignment since *Stage Door*. Producer Erich Pommer, a refugee from Hitler's Germany, had arrived in Hollywood, partnered with actor Charles Laughton, in July 1939. *Dance, Girl, Dance*, based on a story by *Grand Hotel* author Vicki Baum, would be one of his first American films. Maureen O'Hara, Laughton's personal protégée, had been set to star, with Louis Hayward providing the love interest. Pommer considered Lucy ideal for the third-billed role, that of a burlesque queen and rival of O'Hara.

Production commenced in mid-April, but after only a week the

lle Ball was one of several
esses who did *not* land the
ted leading role in *Gone
n the Wind.*

entire cast was unhappy and confused. In response, Pommer fired the original director and brought in Hollywood's foremost female filmmaker, Dorothy Arzner. She reworked the script and sharpened the central conflict between the cultural aspirations of O'Hara and the commercial gold digging of Ball. She further opened up Lucy's character of Bubbles by suggesting she model the role after real-life entertainer, "Texas" Guinan.

Lucy put her all into the role, determined to prove her worth. When the picture opened in October 1940, the New York newspapers rewarded her efforts. Said the *Times:* "It is Miss Ball who brings an occasional zest to the film." The *World Telegram* was more specific in its praise: "The big moment comes when Lucille Ball, as the girl who knows what she wants, does a Hays Office-approved striptease and sings a plaintive song about what is a poor girl to do. It's pretty good, considering that it was censored. It's pretty good even aside from being what it is, because it is just about the only believable sequence in the film." Three thousand miles away, the *Hollywood Reporter* agreed: "Formula plot and poor direction could not keep Lucille Ball from coming out with colors flying. . . . If RKO accomplishes nothing else with this venture, it has informed itself that it has a very important player on the lot in the person of Miss Ball. She has the makings of a star."

Even before the reviews came out, studio executives had taken notice of Lucy's stunning performance. In May, with *Dance, Girl, Dance* only half completed, RKO's new production chief, Harry Edington, announced he would star Lucille Ball in the screen version of the year's Broadway hit, Rodgers and Hart's *Too Many Girls.* The musical concerned the plight of a spoiled heiress whose protective father hires four football players to act as her bodyguards while she is away at college. Naturally, she soon has to protect herself from her protectors! Lucy's pal Ann Miller and actor Richard Carlson were set to co-star, along with various handpicked members of the original Broadway cast.

Director George Abbott arrived in Hollywood from New York in June 1940, bringing with him Eddie Bracken, Hal LeRoy, and a young Cuban musician who had set Broadway hearts aflutter, Desiderio Alberto Arnaz y de Acha—

LB-653A

Lucille Ball, 1939, age twenty-seven.

better known as Desi Arnaz. Ironically, Desi first laid eyes on Lucy as she was coming from filming a brawl scene with Maureen O'Hara for *Dance, Girl, Dance,* and Lucy was decked out in frizzy hair, a painted-on black eye, and a gaudy costume. No one —most of all Lucy and Desi—could have predicted the summer-long romance that was to follow.

With a forty-two-day shooting schedule, *Too Many Girls* actually went before the cameras on July 1, a full week before *Dance, Girl,*

Dance was completed. Carole Lombard, rehearsing Erich Pommer's *They Knew What They Wanted* with Charles Laughton and director Garson Kanin, would occasionally escape the problems on her own picture by visiting Lucy and the exuberant student body of *Too Many Girls'* fictional Pottawottamie College. Neither actress knew that their respective talents were the issue of a heated debate between the RKO front office and the studio's newest producer, Orson Welles. Welles had

been at the studio almost a year but had yet to get a project approved. RKO desperately wanted his "genius," but they also insisted on making the final decisions. The latest bone of contention concerned a project entitled *The Smiler With a Knife,* a detective thriller by English poet Cecil Day Lewis. Welles wished to cast "fresh face" Lucille Ball in the leading role, but RKO wanted an established and bankable star, Miss Lombard. When Carole finally decided to do *Mr. and Mrs.*

Smith for director Alfred Hitchcock, Welles dropped the project, opting to develop another script he was devising with Herman Mankiewicz, the now classic *Citizen Kane.*

Too Many Girls completed principal photography on August 11, and Lucy started work immediately on *A Girl, a Guy, and a Gob,* the first comedy Harold Lloyd produced in which he did not also star. She later recalled the experience of working with the famed comedian: "Watching him every day on the set was an inspiration. His quiet, reassuring knowledge of his art and how to get the job done was something that stuck with me."

George Murphy had the male lead in this farcical tale of love and rewrote much of the script with director Richard Wallace. The two men recognized Lucy's abilities as

Lucille Ball and Richard Dix, *Twelve Crowded Hours,* 1939.

a comedienne and styled the material accordingly. The revised script provided Lucy with some of the best comedy lines of her career to date. Always grateful, Lucy promised Murphy, "Whenever you're out of work, if I'm working, you've got a job with me." (Seventeen years later, after Lucy and Desi had established the largest television operations in town, George took her up on the offer and served a term as vice president of public relations for Desilu Studios, Inc.)

On completion of *A Girl, a Guy, and a Gob*, RKO sent Lucy on a cross-country publicity junket to promote the just released *Dance, Girl, Dance.* Her itinerary included a stopover in New York City for the November 20 premiere of *Too Many Girls.* Lucy arrived at LaGuardia Airport and was greeted by Desi Arnaz, appearing

A

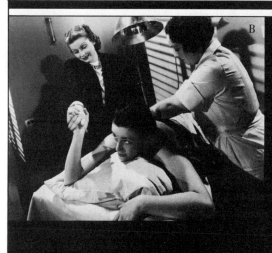

B

A. Headlining *Five Came Back*, (clockwise) Kent Taylor, Lucille Ball, Casey Johnson, Wendy Barrie, and Chester Morris.

B. The *New York Times* suspected Lucy of being "on the verge of giggles" throughout much of *Beauty For the Asking,* certainly not the most credible movie of 1939.

Chester Morris repairs his plane, *The Silver Queen,* downed in the Amazonian jungle.

also one of those years that saw a game of musical chairs being played in the RKO executive suite. The studio had three different production heads within a few short months. Somewhere along the assembly line, *Passage to Bordeaux* was sidetracked.

Replacing it on Lucy's work roster was a rather awful Western adventure, *Valley of the Sun,* with James Craig, Cedric Hardwicke, and Dean Jagger. This mundane potboiler had her cast as a pioneer restaurateur in Arizona during the 1860s. Craig was the virtuous government agent who arrives to save Lucy—and the local Indians—from a villainous Indian agent played by Jagger. The movie, which required location shooting in Taos, New Mexico, completed production November 15, 1941.

Valley of the Sun only served to remind Lucy that RKO had never handled her career properly. But the only alternative—unemployment—was even worse. "I didn't care whether they were 'B' or 'D' pictures," she later confessed with resignation, "as long as I was working."

Carole Lombard, sympathetic to her cause, introduced Lucy to Broadway raconteur Damon Runyon, who had signed on in August as a producer for RKO. Runyon was busy developing one of his own short stories, "Little Pinks," for the screen, and Carole Lombard suggested that Lucy might be ideal for the female lead. Runyon quickly agreed, but when Lucy read the script, she was not so sure herself.

The film, then titled *It Comes Up Love,* would tell the story of a meek busboy (to be played by Henry Fonda, on loan from Fox)

that month with his band at New York's Roxy Theatre. The pair's summertime romance, it seems, had been continued all fall, courtesy of Bell Telephone's long-distance lines. Desi, however, was determined to make their relationship more substantial and, on November 29, popped the all-important question. The next day, the couple eloped to Connecticut.

Later, back in California, the pair purchased a five-acre homestead in Chatsworth, twenty miles north of Hollywood in the San Fernando Valley. Complete with ranch house, stables, a garden, and the obligatory swimming pool, the property was christened "Desilu," the first in a long line of endeavors so labeled.

By March 1941, Lucy and RKO had negotiated a new seven-year contract with a salary increase that she felt would ensure her top-of-the-line material. RKO came up with the cash all right but was less successful finding acceptable scripts.

Look Who's Laughing (originally titled *Look Who's Talking*) was yet another of RKO's attempts to bring to the screen many of the nation's favorite radio stars. This lightweight comedy featured Edgar Bergen and Charlie McCarthy and Jim and Marian Jordan (better known as Fibber McGee and Molly). Despite her new salary, Lucy had only fifth billing, appearing as Bergen's secretary. Screenplay, incidentally, was by James V. Kern who, many years later, would direct a spate of Lucy's television programs. Although the film was completed on June 23, it was held for release until December when, the studio felt, it would provide Christmas-time entertainment. It opened Christmas Eve—seventeen days after the bombing of Pearl Harbor—and did indeed allow audiences a few innocent laughs. The *New York Times* called it "a little holiday blue-plate special," and *Variety* considered Lucy "fetching."

Two weeks before director Allan Dwan had put the finishing touches on *Look Who's Laughing,* producer Erich Pommer *(Dance, Girl, Dance)* announced he intended to give Lucy "the biggest screen role of her career"—the lead in *Passage to Bordeaux,* a serious drama. Robert Stevenson had been engaged to direct the picture, described as "an important film on the studio's 1941–42 program." Unfortunately, 1941 was

A. Happy Birthday, Joan: Lucy helped pal Joan Blondell celebrate her thirtieth birthday on the set of Columbia's *Amazing Mr. Williams*, August 30, 1939.

B. *That's Right, You're Wrong*, featuring bandleader Kay Kyser, was the first of many films starring popular radio performers.

C. Lucy chats with New York's Mayor Fiorello LaGuardia at the annual Film Critics' awards party at the Rainbow Room, January 8, 1940.

The Marines Fly High was Lucy's sixth and last film for RKO's B-picture unit headed by Robert Sisk.

A somber moment in an otherwise wacky film, *You Can't Fool Your Wife,* in which Lucy doubts her husband's fidelity and masquerades as a Latin *senorita* to test him.

Louis Hayward (pictured) portrayed Manhattan playboy, Jimmy Harris, and
Lucille Ball played a wisecracking chorine in *Dance, Girl, Dance*. Robert Wise,
four years away from his directorial debut, edited this 1940 film.

Lucille Ball, *Too Many Girls*, 1940.

who falls in love with a hard-as-nails nightclub singer (Lucy), who is eventually crippled in a fight with her gangster boyfriend. "I've never done *anything* comparable to this," Ball worried. Desi Arnaz, recalling her turmoil in his 1976 memoirs, confided, "It was the only time I'd seen her afraid to tackle a role."

Charles Laughton, who had become something of a business friend, offered to read the script and render an opinion. "Play it!" he insisted. "Play the bitchiest bitch that ever was! Whatever the script calls for. Don't try to soften it!"

With production of the Runyon film delayed until April 1942, Lucy joined Desi in New York, where he was appearing in a revue at Loew's State Theatre. War was declared a couple of weeks later,

Connie Casey and her bodyguards, played by Eddie Bracken, Richard Carlson, Desi Arnaz, and Hal LeRoy.

and the Arnazes rushed home to be with their families. After Christmas, they returned to Loew's with a brand-new husband-and-wife act, including singing, dancing, and amusing dialogue. This was Lucy's first taste of old-time vaudeville, and she loved it!

January 15, 1942, brought sadness to millions when Lucy's pal, Carole Lombard, died in an airplane accident while returning home from an Indiana bond rally. The war had caught the United States industrially unprepared, and various Hollywood celebrities had volunteered to spearhead a national bond drive to raise capital. Carole launched the whole campaign in Ohio, "sold" an unprece-dented $2,017,513 worth of bonds in one day in Indianapolis, but crashed in the plane returning home to California.

The tragedy caused Lucy to cherish her role in the new Damon Runyon picture more than ever. RKO, however, seemed to be up to their old shenanigans. In March, studio chief Charles Koerner de-

Romance blossomed when Desi Arnaz arrived in Hollywood from New York to begin work with Lucille Ball in RKO's *Too Many Girls*.

Back to blond, Lucy's last film in 1940, *A Girl, a Guy and a Gob*, prompted the *New York Times* to write, "Lucille Ball may not be made of India rubber, but she has as much bounce."

Shortly after Lucy's arrival in New York
in November 1940, she was interviewed
by Eleanor Harris for a movie-magazine
article entitled "Why Lucille Ball Prefers
to Remain a Bachelor Girl." Little did
Eleanor know . . .

. . . Lucy and Desi eloped and were wed at the Byram River Beagle Club in Greenwich, Connecticut, November 30, 1940. Photo was taken
only hours later back in Manhattan.

80

At home in Chatsworth.

Happy housewife Lucy admits, "I could have been very happy as an old-fashioned homemaker . . ."

cided to loan Lucy out to 20th Century-Fox for the secondary lead in a new Betty Grable musical, *Strictly Dynamite* (released as *Footlight Serenade*). Fearing Grable's schedule might conflict with Runyon's, Lucy refused the Fox assignment, and RKO suspended her. She spent the next four weeks off salary.

Finally, on April 17, cameras rolled on what Runyon now called *The Big Street*. Directed by Irving Reis, it sported a cast that in-

cluded Agnes Moorehead, Barton MacLane, Hans Conreid, George Cleveland, and Louise Beavers.

By all estimations, *The Big Street* promised to be Lucy's finest film to date. Everyone, especially Lucy, hoped similar assignments would follow, but, as usual, they did not. Dovetailed into the final days of shooting *Street* were setups for Lucy's next feature, a B comedy titled *Seven Days Leave*. Starring Victor Mature (with Lucy receiving second billing),

Seven Days Leave was something of a wartime reworking of that old clinker, *Next Time I Marry.* This time it was Mature who played the prospective heir who has to marry by a certain date in order to collect his legacy. Complicating matters is his hitch in the army and the fact that he can manage only one week's leave. Lucy was cast as his not-so-interested target for romance.

Lucy's lack of enthusiasm for *Seven Days Leave* turned to dis-may when RKO executives cooled their own earlier excitement for *The Big Street.* Runyon had, by mid-summer, left the studio; director Reis had joined the army; the film editor had died in the middle of cutting the picture; Fonda was back at 20th Century-Fox; and RKO was no longer confident of the film's merits.

The Big Street was issued quietly on August 13, 1942, eliciting a review in *Variety* that called Lucy's a "superb performance."

Life magazine agreed: "Not until this summer when she played 'Her Highness' in Damon Runyon's *The Big Street* for RKO did anybody face the truth about Lucille: the girl can really act. As Runyon's tough little crippled night-club queen, Lucille is superb."

While RKO had elected to release *The Big Street* without fanfare, Lucy's performance did not go unnoticed by Arthur Freed, head of MGM's most distinguished production unit. Freed's specialty

"A Couple of Country Squires," Lucy and Desi work and play at their new California ranchette. The acreage, in 1942, was valued at $14,500. Thirty years later, the same property was the site of a multimillion-dollar housing development.

was musicals. He made the best and, in 1942, was preparing a screen version of the Cole Porter hit, *DuBarry Was a Lady.* One look at *The Big Street* convinced Freed that he had found his female star.

RKO's Charlie Koerner had long been concerned about his studio's inability to supply satisfactory material for Lucy. When Freed made overtures, he readily agreed to sell MGM half—and later all—of her contract. She signed the new deal on her thirty-first birthday, August 6, 1942, and moved into the deluxe dressing room once occupied by Norma Shearer when she was queen of the MGM lot.

It had taken nine long years, but Lucy's diligence and hard work had paid off. She had arrived.

Lucy was the love interest, but Charlie McCarthy won everyone's heart in *Look Who's Laughing.*

Lucille Ball and James Craig, *Valley of the Sun*, 1942.

A. On location for *Valley of the Sun*, director George Marshall (center) blocks a scene with Billy Gilbert, James Craig, and Lucille Ball.

B. Little Pinks (Henry Fonda) nurses Gloria Lyons (Lucy) back to life after her boyfriend throws her down a flight of stairs. Nevertheless, Gloria's sarcastic motto remains, "A girl's best friend is a dollar."

C. Pinks's Broadway cronies were played to perfection by Ray Collins and Sam Levene.

Flaunting her feathers, Lucy rehearses her "Fanfare" number for *The Big Street*.

Lucille Ball, 1942.

"Can I make this girl love me in seven days?" ponders Victor Mature. "It would be different if I had two weeks!"

Lucille Ball as Madame DuBarry, 1942.

"More Stars Than There Are in Heaven" was MGM's lyrical motto when Lucille Ball joined its classy assemblage of performers in August 1942. Known for quality as well as quantity, MGM's style of motion pictures had become, over the years, distinctly feminine, a plus for Lucy. True, Clark Gable, Spencer Tracy, and William Powell had built successful careers at Metro, but it was the ladies—Garbo, Shearer, Crawford, Harlow—who set the studio apart from its competitors. When she signed the MGM contract, Lucy's studio "sorority sisters" included Judy Garland, Greer Garson, Lana Turner, Ann Sothern (her old Goldwyn chum), and Katharine Hepburn (also from RKO).

Of the thirty-five pictures MGM had scheduled for 1943, almost half concerned the trauma of war. The rest were comedies, light family dramas, and—the studio's trump card—musicals. One of the most lavish would be *DuBarry Was a Lady*, a fantasy. A smash hit on Broadway in 1939, it told the story of a shy washroom attendant in love with a nightclub singer, who, naturally enough, loves someone else. Hoping to eliminate the other man long enough to win the singer's heart, our hero prepares a drink laced with "knockout" drops—then inadvertently takes

Red Skelton, Lucille Ball, *DuBarry Was a Lady*, 1942.

"Just a perfect blendship . . ." Lucy and Red Skelton jaunt through their purposely corny "Friendship" number from *DuBarry Was a Lady*.

the potion himself. In his dreams, he imagines himself to be the outgoing ladies' man, Louis XV, and his singer to be the voluptuous courtesan, Madame DuBarry.

The concept for *DuBarry Was a Lady* had been developed for the screen a few years earlier, reportedly with Mae West in mind, but Hollywood turned down the vehicle. Instead, Ethel Merman agreed to star in a Broadway version, with Cole Porter songs. Bert Lahr, fresh from his success as the Cowardly Lion in *The Wizard of Oz*, co-starred as the amorous Louis, and together Merman and Lahr kept New York audiences entertained for 408 performances.

In 1941, Arthur Freed opened negotiations to buy the screen rights to an earlier Merman-Porter musical, *Panama Hattie*. Because RKO was also seeking the property (for Ginger Rogers), MGM offered to buy both *Hattie* and *DuBarry* in a package deal for $200,000. *Pan-*

Lucille Ball, 1942.

ama Hattie was rushed into production with Ann Sothern starring, but the overall film was a disappointment. So in 1942, Freed, *wunderkind* of MGM's musical unit, looked beyond the MGM roster and sought out Lucy to headline his *DuBarry* film.

Co-starring in the role created by Bert Lahr would be Red Skeleton, with Gene Kelly, who had come west from Broadway a year earlier for Freed's *For Me and My Gal,* playing Red's competitor. Rags Ragland, Donald Meek, Virginia O'Brien, and Zero Mostel, a young comedian Freed had "dis-

covered" in a New York nightclub, completed the cast.

Three MGM artisans, who were assigned to *DuBarry,* contributed greatly to the future of Lucy's career: Sidney Guilaroff, senior hair stylist, insisted on brightening Lucy's locks for this Technicolor extravaganza. He ran various color tests and one afternoon struck on a bright, carrot-pink shade of henna. "The hair may be brown," he explained, "but her soul is on fire." Lucy liked the new color so much that she adopted it as her trademark.

Charles Walters, who at Gene

Kelly's suggestion had been hired as *DuBarry*'s choreographer, guided Lucy through her various dance routines. They renewed a friendship that had begun a few months earlier when he had served as dance director for Lucy's last RKO film, *Seven Days Leave.* One of the reasons Gene had requested him, however, was that Walters had played Kelly's role in Merman's Broadway company of *DuBarry* and knew the material intimately. A short time later, Walters introduced Lucy to another ex-Broadway hoofer, Jack Donohue, who had been in Hollywood eight

Lucy Goes to War: With comedies like *Thousands Cheer,* Lucille Ball joined dozens of Hollywood stars helping to keep wartime morale high.

years directing Shirley Temple's dance routines at Fox. Walters brought Donohue to MGM, and they both became fixtures with the Freed unit. Twenty years later, Lucy hired Donohue to direct her TV series, and between 1962 and 1980, he fulfilled the task countless times. Once, in 1974, when Jack was working elsewhere, Walters stepped in to direct one of Lucy's CBS specials.

Karl Freund, the Academy Award-winning director of photography assigned to *DuBarry,* was the man Desi Arnaz later engaged to film his wife's earliest television escapades. In his memoirs, Desi recalled Freund as "a great artist. Neither Garbo nor Hepburn would make a picture without Karl. He was a big, fat, jolly man who waddled over the set carrying a Thermos full of martinis and giving orders in his thick German accent. . . . He was a kind and brilliant man."

DuBarry Was a Lady had a ten-week shooting schedule, ending November 6, 1942. MGM, intent on establishing Lucy as one of its top stars, rushed her immediately into Joe Pasternak's production of *Thousands Cheer.*

Originally planned as a small, romantic musical about a soldier (Gene Kelly) and a colonel's daughter (Kathryn Grayson),

Thousands Cheer emerged as an all-star spectacle. Interpolated into the story line, for box office reasons, was an army-camp show featuring nearly every face on the MGM lot. Lucy, Ann Sothern, and Marsha Hunt appeared together in a sketch about a trio of prospective WAVEs being interviewed by a lecherous barber (Frank Morgan) posing as the camp physician.

Other "guest stars" in the film included Judy Garland, Mickey Rooney, Eleanor Powell, Red Skelton, Lena Horne, Margaret O'-Brien, June Allyson, Gloria DeHaven, Virginia O'Brien, and Donna Reed.

Among the missing was Metro's blond bombshell, Lana Turner, who had recently become pregnant

With the Boys Away . . . women had to take over various essential jobs. Lucy demonstrates such atypical feminine duties as taking coins at a tollgate, driving a taxicab, and pumping gas.

with daughter Cheryl. Freed, unaware of Lana's condition, sent her a copy of the script for his newest musical venture, *Best Foot Forward.* When Lana sent her regrets, Freed offered the starring role to Lucy. A "prep school" musical, *Best Foot Forward* had many things in common with *Too Many Girls.* For one thing, both properties originated as Broadway shows staged by George Abbott. Hugh Martin and Ralph Blane, vocal arrangers for *Girls,* wrote the score for *Forward,* and MGM, like RKO,

had enough faith in the Broadway cast to import many of Abbott's performers for their film version: June Allyson, Nancy Walker, Tommy Dix, Gil Stratton, Kenny Bowers, and Jack Jordan.

Best Foot Forward told the charming story of a young cadet (Tommy Dix) who invites a Hollywood starlet (Lucy) to be his date at the Winsocki school prom, never dreaming that she would say yes. A Hollywood press agent recognizes the invitation as an excellent promotional gimmick and convinces his star to accept. No one stops to consider the reaction of the youth's jealous girl friend.

Former musical-comedy actor Eddie Buzzell, who had recently directed MGM movies starring the Marx Brothers and one with Red Skelton, directed *Forward* in early

A. "All America's Clicking!" reads the poster, and Lucy joins in, knitting "something for the boys."

B. No task too trivial, Lucy helps collect scrap metal, supports the Bundles for Bluejackets fund, and demonstrates (for national advertisements) the proper usage of V-Mail stationery.

Typecast Again! Lucille Ball portrays an actress named Lucille Ball, who gets talked into attending a military school prom by her conniving press agent (William Gaxton) in MGM's *Best Foot Forward*.

1943. Shooting alongside *Best Foot Forward* on another MGM sound stage was the Dory Schary-Irving Starr production of *Bataan*, directed by Tay Garnett. Appearing in a featured role, as a young soldier dying of malaria, was Desi Arnaz.

Lucy took her first "vacation" after nearly a year of nonstop filmmaking in April–May 1943. Some of that free time was utilized catching up on a favorite pastime: radio. Lucy not only listened to it, she also took an active role in it, appearing as a guest on such programs as "Lady Esther Presents Orson Welles," "Screen Guild Theatre," "Blue Ribbon Town," and "The Al Jolson Show." But as her vacation came to a close, she had more to worry about than just a new film—husband Desi had been drafted!

Luckily, Desi would spend much of the war in Southern California, stationed at the Army's Birmingham General Hospital located only a few miles from the Arnaz ranch. He was assigned to Special Services and organized entertainment for wounded servicemen arriving stateside from the South Pacific. Lucy lent a hand, often enlisting the aid of her talented Hollywood co-workers.

Meet the People was the title of Lucy's new Freed production, and as work got underway in June, the fruits of previous MGM labors arrived on the screen. First to premiere (June 3) was Desi's *Bataan*, hailed by some critics as the finest war film of the year. *Best Foot Forward*, due for national release in October, opened in a special engagement June 29—and the critics raved. The *New York Times* called it "a rollicking musical film which pops with hilarious situations,

Hell hath no fury . . . as Lucille Ball finds out when the girl friend (Virginia Weidler) of Lucy's prom date (Tommy Dix) enters the picture.

sparkling dialogue and the fresh spirit of youth."

DuBarry Was a Lady opened August 13, with critic Bosley Crowther leading the cheers: "Metro has given it the luster of a million dollars in gold," he wrote, adding, "They have tossed the juicy dame role to Lucille Ball, who carries it well." *Thousands Cheer,* in which Lucy did a cameo sketch, opened in New York September 13, with proceeds from the first night's special benefit performance going to the Third War Loan Drive. The box office took in $534,000 that evening, and MGM reaped equally bankable notices in the next day's papers.

Meet the People started production June 7, 1943. In it, Lucy portrayed an actress who takes a job in a Delaware shipyard with the dual purpose of "meeting the people" (for a publicity stunt) and dealing with the playwright (Dick Powell) who has refused to cast her in his new play. Virginia O'Brien, Bert Lahr, Rags Ragland, and June Allyson (who met future husband Powell here) had featured roles. Like many of Freed's musicals, *People* was based on a Broadway show. The fact that everyone had apparently overlooked, however, was that the Broadway version had not been much of a success. When the two-month production ended in July, few studio executives still professed fondness for the film. Only the songs, like "In Times Like These," seemed to have any pizzazz.

Unfortunately, there were no new assignments for Lucy waiting in the wings to blunt the negative effects of *Meet the People.* Freed was busy with *The Harvey Girls, Girl Crazy,* and *Meet Me in St. Louis,* projects for Judy Garland, and none contained roles suited to Lucy. The only hope she had was that Freed would be able to sell the

front office on his ambitious plan to stage an all-star film version of the *Ziegfeld Follies.*

In the meantime, Lucy spent the autumn and winter months of 1943–44 shuttling between a tiny office at MGM in Culver City and the network radio studios of CBS and NBC, clustered in the heart of Hollywood. During that period, she appeared on at least thirteen major network broadcasts, often in better roles than she had ever gotten in the movies. She starred in *My Sister Eileen* on "Philip Morris Playhouse," *The Case of the Blue Blood Stain* on "The Orson Welles Show," and *A Night to Remember* on "Screen Guild Players." She guest-starred on Bing Crosby's "Kraft Music Hall" three times (once to promote *DuBarry*) and appeared on "The Abbott and Costello Show," "The Jack Carson Show," and, in a feast of one-liners, "The Burns 'n' Allen Show."

At MGM, she shared a tiny cubicle with two other contractees who were drawing few assignments that year from the top brass: veteran director Edward Sedgwick, whose style was considered "incurably old-fashioned," and Buster Keaton, one of Sedgwick's —and the world's—greatest clowns. The trio also shared their troubles, occasionally talked in depth about various styles of comedy (Keaton reportedly taught Lucy the importance of detail to a good comedy performance), and, as the weeks wore on, began building "Rube Goldberg-type" machines out of pencils, string, and rubber bands.

Lucy's career anxieties were abated on January 9 when Freed announced that *Ziegfeld Follies of 1944* would go before the cameras March 1, with a staggering $3 million budget. The picture, like Ziegfeld's opulent stage shows, would be a variety revue, *sans* story. Ini-

Buckle Down, Winsocki!: Winsocki military academy will never be the same after Lucy's surprise visit.

tial plans called for twenty segments (musical numbers and sketches), to involve every major MGM star. Several classic comedy routines had been dusted off, and every writer at the studio was being called upon to supply additional material. Vincente Minnelli was asked to co-direct and paste together the film.

Lucy was set to star in four segments—the traditional opening number that would "bring on" the Ziegfeld girls, plus three music-and-comedy numbers to be slotted later within the movie. Freed, however, was constantly revising his inventory, and by the time Lucy's opener went into rehearsal on April 18, 1944, the latter three sketches had been scrubbed. Gone were "Glorifying the American Girl," which would have teamed Lucy with Marilyn Maxwell, Lucille Bremer, and Lena Horne; "Fireside Chat," with Judy Garland and Ann Sothern; and "A Trip to Hollywood," with Jimmy Durante and Miss Maxwell.

What remained was "Here's to the Girls," featuring Fred Astaire singing "Bring on the Beautiful Girls" while Virginia O'Brien countered with "Bring on the Beautiful Men." The entire sequence had a circus motif, with the girls appearing on a merry-go-round, riding *live* white horses. (Lucy's steed was none other than Silver, famed mount of the Lone Ranger.) As the number progresses, Lucy steps from her horse, cracks a rhinestone-studded whip, and proceeds to "tame" eight writhing dancers, dressed in stunning black-sequined panther suits.

Lucy's outfit, all in pink, was the brainchild of designer Helen Rose, who later recalled, "I created lavish outfits of pink sequins, using twelve hundred ostrich feathers. With Lucille Ball's flaming red hair, I thought it was the best number in the picture."

Regarding her strangely tinted hair, Lucy told the press, "This orange color isn't natural. But it looks good in Technicolor, so why should I kick? Besides, I'm just living up to Hollywood's idea of a showgirl." Perhaps without knowing it, Lucy had explained why the earlier stream of roles she was getting at MGM had slowed to a trickle—a studio had again cast her as a showgirl. The *Ziegfeld* assignment was, after all, no more than another Goldwyn bit.

Ziegfeld Follies did allow Lucy the opportunity to renew some old acquaintances. Shooting concurrently with "Here's to the Ladies" was "Baby Snooks and the Burglars," a comedy routine starring Fanny Brice—who was also preparing a second sketch, "The Sweepstakes Ticket," with character actor William Frawley. This movie was Fanny's first film in nearly a decade. Her career, which dated back to vaudeville and the original *Ziegfeld Follies*, had by 1944 become almost exclusively radio. Now back at MGM, she spent many production breaks chatting with Lucy and her other co-stars. Neither of these two "funny ladies" could know that one of

Lucy Visits *Bataan*—on a sound stage at MGM, that is! Surrounding her on the set of Tay Garnett's war epic are Barry Nelson, Lee Bowman, Lloyd Nolan, George Murphy . . . and a slightly jealous Desi Arnaz.

Fanny's radio writers, Jess Oppenheimer, would have a profound influence on Lucy's own radio and television career several years later.

By the time *Ziegfeld Follies* finished shooting, Lucy had come to realize that if she were to triumph at MGM, it would have to be outside the Freed unit. Taking her career into her own hands once

Bert Lahr plays the comedic commodore of a houseboat, which Lucille Ball prepares to christen in an amusing ceremony in MGM's version of *Meet the People.*

again, she began scouting the lot for a good role. A promising part came up in a new William Powell movie, *The Hoodlum Saint,* but Lucy lost it to Angela Lansbury. (The loss proved to be a gain when *Saint* lost its halo at the box office.)

Salvation arrived in the guise of *Without Love,* the third MGM romantic teaming of Katharine Hepburn and Spencer Tracy. Lucy and Keenan Wynn won co-starring roles as the film's comic relief, and both benefited greatly. Lucy portrayed a real estate broker, Kitty Trimbell, a mistress of the wry remark. Donald Ogden Stewart's script, based on the stage play by Philip Barry, provided Lucy with some marvelously effective lines, and when the picture was released in March 1944, not a critic failed to notice. Said James Agee, "It is good to see Lucille Ball doing so well with a kind of role new to her." *Time* magazine concurred: "Lucille Ball handles her lowly wise-cracks so well as to set up a new career for herself." The *New York World-Telegram* announced, "Every time Lucille Ball strolls in

Lucille Ball, 1943.

Lucy woos Dick Powell, the playwright who done her wrong in *Meet the People*.

to drench the place with acid wit, it's a pleasure." And Harrison Carroll, of the *Los Angeles Herald-Express*, summed it all up as "Lucille's best work on the screen."

Meet the People, the Dick Powell musical, tiptoed quietly into theatres in September 1944, while *Without Love* was still shooting. When the reviews came out, Arthur Freed's worst fears were realized. The *New York Times* heralded the film: "Iron Ships, Wooden Plot." Luckily, critics did not blame the cast for the film's lethargy, and Lucy received surprisingly good notices. The *Hollywood Reporter* commented, "Lucille Ball, whose versatile talents seem to brighten with every appearance, gives just about her best all-around performance to date and never looked lovelier."

Looking lovely was just about all that was required for her next MGM assignment, a cameo in *Bud Abbott and Lou Costello in Hollywood* (the *only* Metro title ever to include any star's *full* name). Long on title, short on plot, the film found the zany duo on the loose at fictional Mammoth Studios. Lucille Ball appeared as herself in a movie-within-a-movie in production during Bud and Lou's visit.

On November 1, 1944, MGM "sneaked" *Ziegfeld Follies of 1944* at Westwood Village Theatre in Los Angeles with disastrous results. Retakes and added scenes were ordered, but a second preview several months later enchanted few. A road-show premiere was held in Boston in August 1945, but audience reaction proved to be so cool that MGM withdrew the movie for yet another seven months. It was ultimately released in April 1946, retitled—appropriately—*Ziegfeld Follies of 1946.*

In March 1945, Lucy won the third lead (behind Van Johnson

Lucy's frequent radio appearances brought her into contact with such performers as Chet Huntley, the thirty-one-year-old narrator of CBS's "I Was There" drama series.

and Esther Williams) in *Easy to Wed*, a musical comedy remake of the 1937 film, *Libeled Lady*. Lucy and Van had been friends for years, he having come to Hollywood with Desi for *Too Many Girls;* no subsequent film offers followed the RKO musical, and by late 1941, Van was ready to give up and go home. The Arnazes took him to dinner at Chasen's where the trio ran into talent scout Billy Grady. "Billy, this kid *can't* go back to New York!" pleaded Lucy. "Stop by MGM on your way to the depot," Grady advised, and a twelve-year relationship between Johnson and MGM was launched.

In 1944, Van and Esther Williams had wowed audiences in Joe Pasternak's musical, *Thrill of Romance*, and as a follow-up, Jack Cummings had prepared *Easy to Wed*. Eddie Buzzell, Lucy's pal from *Best Foot Forward*, was set as director, and Jack Donohue as choreographer. Keenan Wynn, who had played so beautifully with Lucy in *Without Love*, would be reunited with her in the new film. It was like "old home week," and the participants responded accordingly. The day after Donohue started the grueling dance rehearsals, Lucy decided to even the score. She showed up on the set in a wheelchair, one of her arms in a

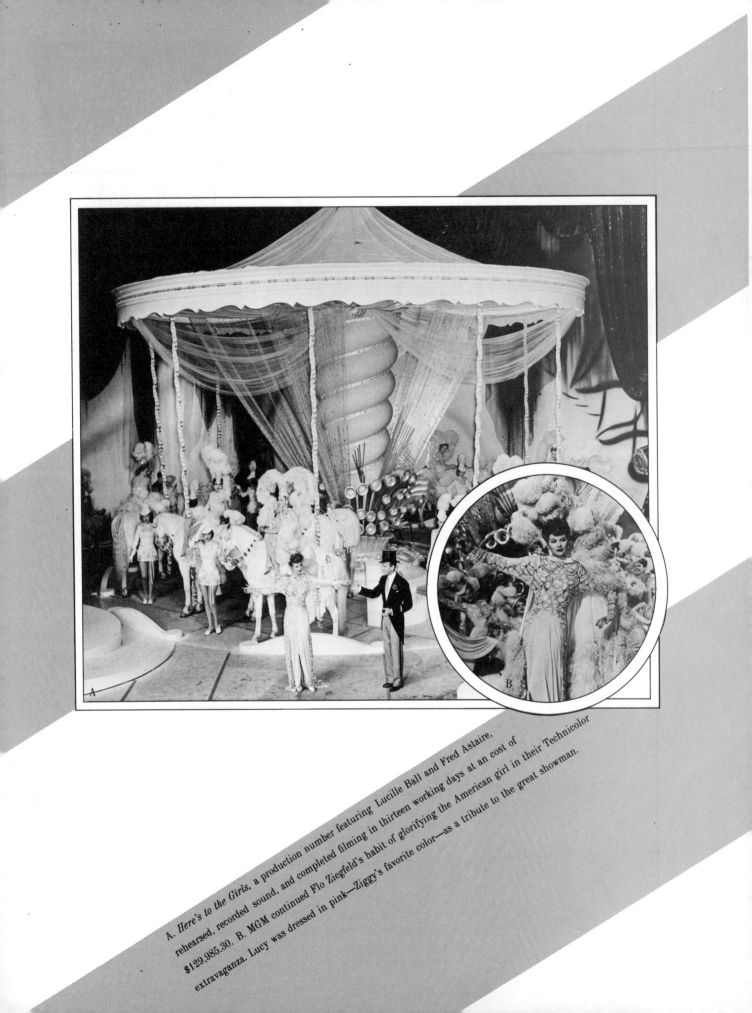

A. *Here's to the Girls*, a production number featuring Lucille Ball and Fred Astaire, rehearsed, recorded sound, and completed filming in thirteen working days at an cost of $129,985.30. B. MGM continued Flo Ziegfeld's habit of glorifying the American girl in their Technicolor extravaganza. Lucy was dressed in pink—Ziggy's favorite color—as a tribute to the great showman.

Lucille Ball, Ziegfeld Follies, 1944.

A. Surprise comedy team of the year, Lucy and Keenan Wynn amused audiences so much in *Without Love* that Metro decided to feature them in a second film—pronto!

B. Contemplating a marriage "without love," scientist Spencer Tracy seeks advice from his real estate agent, Lucille Ball.

Lucy and Desi dance at Ciro's during one of his weekend furloughs.

It's what's between the ears that counts, and Lucy, in a dumb-Dora role created by Jean Harlow, proved to Van Johnson that there wasn't much.

Sergeant and Mrs. Desi Arnaz attend the Los Angeles premiere of *White Cliffs of Dover*, presented as a benefit for the Volunteer Army Canteen Service.

sling, her teeth blacked out, her hair tousled, and her cheek artificially bruised. She held up a homemade sign: "I am not working for Donohue . . . Period." But work she did.

Van Johnson recreated William Powell's role in *Libeled Lady*. Miss Williams supplanted Myrna Loy; Lucy, Jean Harlow; and Wynn, Spencer Tracy. The plot concerned an editor (Wynn) whose newspaper mistakenly accuses a socialite (Williams) of husband-stealing. She threatens a lawsuit, and to save the paper he concocts a scheme to have his own fiancée

(Lucy) pose as a friend's (Johnson's) wife, and to have that friend become involved with the outraged socialite. Hence, he could prove that the lady was indeed dallying with a married man. Obviously, there are complications along the way, all adding to the film's hilarity. When production ended June 26, 1945, everyone was sure MGM had another winner.

The war in Europe ended May 8, 1945; the Japanese surrendered August 14; and on November 16, Desi Arnaz was discharged. Desi, like countless other GIs, had had an opportunity during his tour of

A peck on the cheek was small payment for the wacky problems Keenan Wynn and Van Johnson created for Lucy in *Easy to Wed.*

Lou Costello offers unwanted advice as a harried Robert Leonard attempts to shoot a love scene with Lucy and Preston Foster.

Lucy played Ricki, a beautiful con artist in love with fellow crook, John Hodiak, in *Two Smart People.*

duty to reevaluate his "priorities." One thing Arnaz had decided was that making movies was not his cup of tea. After *Too Many Girls*, RKO had been able to find only mediocre properties in which to feature his Latin persona. *Bataan* had brought him to MGM in 1943, but they too had little to offer in the way of career-building parts. Getting out of the service, Arnaz opted to terminate his Metro contract and devote his time to music.

Lucy also decided to pack her bags to leave MGM that autumn, but for precisely the opposite reason: she wanted desperately to *make* films—good films—but MGM, like RKO before it, had become more of a hindrance than a help. In October 1945, Lucy started work on what would be her last picture under her MGM contract. *Time for Two,* soon retitled *Two Smart People*, told the bittersweet story of two con artists (Lucy and John Hodiak) who fall in love on a train taking him off to prison. Lloyd Nolan portrayed the dutiful cop, and wiry Elisha Cook, Jr., was a thief trying to find the counterfeit plates Hodiak has stolen. Only mildly entertaining, the movie wasted the talents of the entire company. After production was completed on November 15, Lucy joined Desi in bidding MGM a fond adieu.

Free-lancing (working for oneself, one project at a time, without a studio contract) was the wave of Hollywood's future, but in 1945, it was still a pretty risky business. Lucy, however, was sure she could fend for herself. Bolstering her confidence was the knowledge that she had already been offered a job.

Lucille Ball.

Lucy, The Comedy Star

Happy-go-lucky fashion designer Lucy sees red in more places than her hair when she discovers that hubby George Brent has been two-timing her in *Lover Come Back.*

Striking out on her own in late 1945, Lucille Ball was reminded of the importance of past associations, the result of her propensity for making and keeping friends within the industry. One of those friends was Fred Kohlmar, the man who first brought her to Hollywood in 1933 when he was a talent agent for Sam Goldwyn. Kohlmar, who had since become a producer at 20th Century-Fox, called Lucy during her final weeks at MGM and invited her to co-star with Mark Stevens and Clifton Webb in *The Dark Corner,* a Leo Rosten mystery. The film concerned an ex-con private eye (Stevens) who finds himself framed for a murder. His secretary (Lucy) helps him dodge the police long enough to find the real killer (Webb). The distinguished Henry Hathaway directed.

Murder mysteries were not typical Lucy fare, so on the first day of filming, she was admittedly nervous. Her first scene called for her to be behind a desk, typing. During the lunch break, the director noticed what it was that she had typed. The paper, still in the machine, read: "Dear Mr. Hathaway, If you knew how—— nervous I was today you wouldn't dare shoot the picture and you would call the whole thing off and then you wou. . . ." Further down the sheet were the words,

Lucille Ball, age thirty-four.

"Lucy is a sissy. Lucy is a sissy. Lucy is a sissy."

When the "sissy" returned to the set for the afternoon scenes, she found a new piece of paper in the typewriter. On it was typed, "Dear Lucy, Would it help you to know that I'm nervous as hell myself? Love, H. H."

The Dark Corner filmed for nearly three months, wrapping March 15, 1946. Lucy had finished her scenes a few weeks earlier, reporting immediately for work at Universal in *Lover Come Back*. Originally titled *Lesson in Love*, this light romantic comedy seemed to be more in keeping with Lucy's usual style in pictures. William A. Seiter, another old friend who had guided her through *Roberta* and *Room Service* at RKO, was director.

George Brent co-starred in *Lover Come Back* as a returning veteran who faces a divorce when his wife (Lucy) discovers that he spent the last few months in the cozy company of a shapely female war photographer (Vera Zorina). The film finished production April 6, and Lucy, wanting to spend some time with Desi, started a self-imposed six-month sabbatical from pictures. Desi entertained with his rhumba band throughout

the spring at Ciro's, a popular Los Angeles night spot and, in July, took the band to New York's Copacabana. Lucy went along for the opening. A national road tour followed, and while Lucy could not visit every city, her brother Fred could—Desi had hired him to be his road manager.

The summer of 1946, like that of '43, was something of a "Lucille Ball Film Festival": three of her movies were released. First out was *The Dark Corner,* opening May 8. The picture itself was cited as surprisingly good, but the reviews clearly belonged to Lucy. "Miss Ball is tops," quipped *Variety.* The *Los Angeles Examiner* was more verbose: "In the acting department, Lucille Ball is entitled to heavy honors. When this young lady is given half a chance, she demonstrates a quality of work that is all too rare in pictures. She has been given ample opportunity in this to display her superior ability."

Lover Come Back, finished in April, was rushed into theatres June 19, possibly to capitalize on the favorable reception afforded *Dark Corner.* The Universal comedy would certainly have trouble winning any of its own; critics labeled the film a "dud," but seemed more than willing to applaud its star. The *Los Angeles Times* said: "Miss Ball reveals light comedy talents of better than average quality," while the *Hollywood Reporter* went so far as to say, "Lucille Ball, never lovelier, . . . plays the wife for a riot."

When *Easy to Wed* opened July 11, The *New York Times* labeled Lucy and Keenan Wynn "the best things" about the picture, and the *Los Angeles Times* indicated that her comedy scenes were "the most compensating feature. . . . She is at her super best." Dorothy Manners, writing in the *Los Angeles Exam-*

Killing time in a penny arcade, Lucy and Mark Stevens keep an eye out for both the police and the villains in *The Dark Corner*.

iner, confessed, "I've never been an ardent fan of Lucy's, but here she changes my mind. She is a thoroughly delectable dish. . . ." *Cue* magazine found Lucy's performance hysterically funny: "She steals every scene she plays, and has two howlers: one, in which she learns how to answer a drake's mating call to his duck; and two, in which she plays a livid lady in the grand Bernhardt manner. That skit is the prize of the year!"

Prize, indeed. Lucy and fellow redhead Danny Kaye (starring in films for Goldwyn) were named "King and Queen of Comedy—1946" by the Associated Drama Guild of America. MGM nearly choked on Lucy's good fortunes and second-guessed the wisdom of letting her leave. Returning to the "lion's den," however, was the farthest thing from Lucy's mind. October brought the new radio season and with it, guest appearances on "The Eddie Cantor Show," Jack Carson's "Sealtest Village Store," and "The Bob Hope Show," of which husband Desi was now the musical director.

In November, Lucy started work on her sixtieth (yes, sixtieth!) motion picture, another Leo Rosten thriller, *Personal Column,* released as *Lured.* Based on an earlier French film starring Maurice Chevalier, *Lured* was produced by James Nasser, who headquartered his operations at a small, independent facility he owned in Hollywood known as General Service Studios. Douglas Sirk, soon to win fame for his lush romantic pictures at Universal, directed. The cast included George Sanders, Charles Coburn, Boris Karloff, Alan Mowbray, and Cedric Hardwicke. As these names suggest, the picture was set in London where

Lucy portrayed an American showgirl—what else?—who finds herself stranded in England when her show folds. One of her roommates disappears, then turns up dead, after answering an ad in a newspaper's "personal column," and Scotland Yard enlists Lucy's aid in trapping the killer. She is to be the "bait," answering such ads as "Bird lover wants attractive young woman, unattached, as soul mate," and "Bookworm seeks beautiful book-lover to help catalogue library."

Lured was completed January 10, 1947, and without missing a beat, Lucy reported to her old alma mater, Columbia, after a twelve-year absence, to begin *Her Husband's Affairs,* a light comedy directed by S. Sylvan Simon, a friend from MGM. Franchot Tone co-starred, and the supporting cast included Edward Everett Horton and Gene Lockhart. Franchot and Lucy portrayed a husband-and-wife team of advertising specialists who agree to promote a new hair remover—not knowing that the cream, instead, *grows* hair! One scene, in which unsuspecting customers attempt to use the product for "waterless shaving," ends with some 250 people sporting fluffy new beards.

An equally funny predicament cropped up off camera. The arch-conservative Hollywood Code Office, in a move to keep S-E-X off the screen, had outlawed the use of double beds in movies— even if the occupants were clearly identified as husband and wife. Twin beds, however, created production problems—a husband, for instance, could never give his wife a good-night kiss, unless, of course, he possessed lips of Ubangi proportions. For *Her Husband's*

Affairs, Columbia craftsmen tried to circumvent the clumsy bed issue by creating the "Hollywood bed," which was nothing more than two twin beds shoved together and joined by a common headboard. The Code Office reluctantly approved, but later, when the picture was sent abroad, the British Board of Film Censors found the bed "offensive." The scenes had to be reshot—at great expense—with the two twin beds spread exactly eighteen inches apart!

Lucy's last film for MGM, *Two Smart People,* finally made it to the theatres in December 1946, but it had hardly been worth the wait. The *New York Times* lamented, "Lucille Ball is painfully defeated by the script at almost every turn," and called the film "a dreadfully boring hodgepodge."

The spring of 1947 found Lucy on network radio at least once a week. She co-starred with Bob Hope and Frank Sinatra in *Too Many Husbands* (for "Screen Guild Players"), and did *The Lion and the Mouse* for "Reader's Digest—Radio Edition." On May 27, Bob Hope broadcast his weekly outing "on location" from Detroit, and, with Desi going along to conduct the orchestra, Lucy appeared as a guest on the program.

In June, Lucy herself took to the road, starting a six-month tour in the Harold Kennedy-Herbert Kenwith production of Elmer Rice's play, *Dream Girl.* Jus Addis directed, and Scott McKay, Hayden Rorke, and Barbara Morrison were featured. A comedic blend of reality and fantasy, *Dream Girl* was something of a female version of the "Walter Mitty" tale, about the very vivid daydreams of a young bookshop proprietress. The play

B

opened June 10 at the McCarter Theatre in Princeton, New Jersey, where Lucy had played in *Hey Diddle Diddle* more than a decade before, toured the country, then closed in January at the Biltmore Theatre in Los Angeles when Lucy came down with a virus. Of her opening night, one Los Angeles critic raved: "Here is a young lady of the films who could . . . have a dazzling footlight career. . . . Miss Ball has efficiency as a comedienne. She can tinge a scene delicately with pathos and has special

A. First Lesson in Makeup: Pamela Ball, Lucy's niece (brother Fred's daughter), gets some firsthand information in the art of cosmetics in her aunt's dressing room at Universal.

B. Happy New Year: Lucy and Desi welcomed in 1946 with champagne and the traditional noisemakers at Ciro's, a popular Hollywood night spot.

facility in dealing with sharp-edged repartee."

In August, United Artists released *Lured,* and in November Columbia issued *Her Husband's Affairs.* Both films received only lukewarm reviews, but—as had become the custom—Lucy was

Lucy on the radio, 1946.

Meet Miss Helicopter! Selected as "The Helicopter Girl of 1946," Lucy surveys a model of a new twenty-seven-passenger whirlybird.

well liked. Regarding her serio-comic role in the former, the *Hollywood Citizen News* told readers, "Miss Ball, never a dull comedienne, makes the most of the role —to the benefit of the picture and pleasure of the audience." The *New York Times* called it "a sturdy performance," and *Cue* magazine labeled her "a priceless comedienne."

After viewing *Her Husband's Affairs*, John Maynard of the *New York Journal-American* wrote, "Lucille Ball reasserts very firmly that she is about the best comedienne Hollywood has to offer. Miss Ball is a pleasure, that's what she is. . . ." *Life* paid her perhaps the ultimate compliment: "Good looking Lucille Ball, as the wife, could give any actress lessons on

how to play comedy, and will remind many of Carole Lombard at her best."

The reviews did not go unnoticed by Lucy's pal Bob Hope, who, with producer Robert Welch, was planning a remake of Damon Runyon's story, "Little Miss Marker." Lucy would play Gladys O'Neill, a nightclub singer who has a love-hate relationship with a shady Broadway bookie, Sorrowful Jones (Hope). Their lives are complicated when a gambler leaves his little girl as collateral for a bet— then kills himself when his horse loses.

Under Sidney Lanfield's direction, production on the Hope picture ended June 9, 1948, the day after Bob's buddy Milton Berle started a new show, "The Texaco

Star Theatre," not on radio, but on that other device—television. Hollywood was fearful that the new medium might infringe on movie box-office receipts.

Network radio, however, was still alive and kicking that summer. Arthur Godfrey had suddenly caught on with his weekly CBS "Talent Scouts" program, and Eve Arden, Hollywood's favorite second banana, was sharpening her tongue in anticipation of her new school teacher role in "Our Miss Brooks." And in June 1948, Lucille Ball began rehearsals for the pilot of a projected husband-and-wife radio comedy, "My Favorite Husband."

Based on characters created by Isabel Scott Rorick in two successful novels, "My Favorite Husband" was adapted for radio by Frank Fox and Bill Davenport, a pair of "Ozzie and Harriet" scribes. CBS executives decided to put the pilot on the air as a one-shot "special" Monday, July 5. Lucy would star as Liz, the slightly scatterbrained but not dumb wife

Lucille Ball and George Sanders, *Lured*, 1946.

A. Goodnight kisses were not allowed in 1946, and this scene was ultimately altered in the release print of *Her Husband's Affairs*.

B. Champagne for Two: Lucille Ball and Edward Everett Horton drink to each other's health in this scene from Columbia's *Her Husband's Affairs*.

C. Lucille Ball and Lela Bliss, *Dream Girl*, 1947.

D. The Lady Is a Tramp—at least in her fantasies. Lucy portrayed Georgina Allerton, a daydreaming bookstore owner in Elmer Rice's *Dream Girl*.

of George Cugat, fifth vice president of a midwestern bank. With Lee Bowman cast opposite Lucy, the pilot elicited such favorable comments—from the public and critics alike—that CBS announced a regular "My Favorite Husband" series that would premiere later that month. *Variety* called the special "reminiscent of the better drawing-room comedies in legit and early Capra pix."

One week after the pilot broadcast, Lucy returned to her old stomping grounds, RKO, to begin work on a new film, *Easy Living*, in which she was paired with Victor Mature, her *Seven Days Leave* co-star. Mature played a professional football star, torn between slowing down because of a possible heart condition and pushing ahead to satisfy his status-conscious wife (Lizabeth Scott). Lucy was cast as the understanding "other woman," secretary to the team manager, played by Lloyd Nolan.

Also in the film, portraying a sports reporter, was a young comedian named Jack Paar. One day, Lucy and producer Robert Sparks were watching some rushes when the redhead began to talk about her new radio show. Lee Bowman, it seemed, would not be continuing as husband George. "Jack," she asked, "do you know any young actor who does light comedy like you do in this role who would want to play opposite me in a new radio series?" Jack suggested a

couple of friends, Hal March and
Hy Averback, only later realizing
that Lucy had, in a rather round-
about fashion, been asking if Jack
himself were interested.

"My Favorite Husband" took to
the air as a weekly radio series Fri-
day, July 23, 1948, with Gordon
Hughes producing and directing.
Richard Denning had been cast as
Lucy's husband, with Gale Gordon
and Bea Benadaret in supporting
roles. Fox and Davenport provided
the first ten scripts, enough to take
the program through its initial
summer run. In September, however, they had to report back to
Ozzie Nelson and family, so CBS
assigned two of its staff writers,
Bob Carroll, Jr., and Madelyn
Pugh, to take over. For Bob and
Madelyn, this was the beginning of
a wonderful working relationship
with Lucille Ball.

Lucy's antics as Liz Cugat did
not go unnoticed by director S.
Sylvan Simon who had last worked
with Lucy on *Her Husband's
Affairs.* Since completing that
movie, Simon had borrowed Red
Skelton from MGM and put together a slapstick sensation called
The Fuller Brush Man, which was
a spectacular success. Columbia
Pictures asked Simon to come up
with sequels, but Skelton was
under contract to MGM. That was
when Simon thought of Lucy. Her
recent work in *Affairs, Dream Girl,*
and *My Favorite Husband* convinced him that she would be ideal

A and B. Under the big top, Lucy and Desi performed with the Ringling Brothers and Barnum and Bailey circus in Hollywood during a charity benefit for St. John's Hospital, September 5, 1948.

C. Lucille Ball and Bob Hope during the production of *Sorrowful Jones* for Paramount.

D. Lloyd Nolan gives Lucy advice on not falling for a married football player in RKO's *Easy Living*.

for a series of Skelton-like comedies. He made her an offer, and she signed a contract in late 1948 to make three Columbia pictures at a handsome $85,000 each, with the stipulation that she could continue her radio work.

While "My Favorite Husband" continued to delight millions, an important personnel change had occurred at the studio. Producer-director Gordon Hughes had resigned, and CBS replaced him with veteran comedy writer Jess Oppenheimer who took over Hughes's responsibilities and also became the program's head writer. Oppenheimer's first creative decision was to make the Cugat characters more identifiable to the average person. To that end, the Cugats became the more WASP-ish Coopers, and while George continued to be a banker, the crises in the couple's lives became more domestic. Jess also helped Lucy to learn to "loosen up," to be more animated in her delivery. In fact, he surprised her one week by handing her a pair of tickets to the next Jack Benny broadcast. Benny, Jess knew, performed—even when on

the radio—using a vast array of mannerisms and physical business. Lucy used the tickets, observed Benny in action, and agreed that such technique would greatly improve her radio show.

In February 1949, Lucy began dividing her time between CBS and Columbia's studios where she was shooting the first of the three Simon comedies, *Miss Grant Takes Richmond,* the story of a dim-witted secretary (Lucy) who takes a job with a real estate agent (William Holden) who is secretly running a bookmaking operation in his back room. Production was completed within two months.

On June 5, Paramount released *Sorrowful Jones,* and within weeks it had done twice as much business as any previous Bob Hope comedy. Lucy, likewise, won excellent notices, including this one in the *Los Angeles Times:* "Lucille Ball is a slick choice for the feminine lead, interpreting the author's idea of a sophisticated yet warmhearted Broadway nightclub singer skillfully." Hoping lightning could strike twice, Paramount immediately engaged Lucy to co-star with Hope in *Fancy Pants,* scheduled to begin filming in August.

Originally titled *When Men Were Men, Fancy Pants* was actually a remake of the 1935 Charles Laughton comedy, *Ruggles of Red Gap.* Lucy portrayed a nouveau riche lass from New Mexico who, while traveling in Europe, meets an American actor-turned-English butler (Hope). Returning with her to the states, Hope tries to pass himself off as an English nobleman, much to the disbelief of Lucy's gun-toting boyfriend (Bruce Cabot). The comedy was directed by George Marshall from a screenplay by Edmund Hartmann and Robert O'Brien.

The new season of "My Favorite Husband" began September 2, 1949, with Liz Cooper trying to find a recipe that calls for twenty-four quarts of sour milk—the milk that she forgot to discontinue before leaving on vacation. Jess Oppenheimer's tactic of involving his characters in "exaggerated everyday problems" kept "Husband" near the top of the ratings throughout the 1949–50 radio season.

In the meantime, both *Miss Grant Takes Richmond* and *Easy Living* opened, and the sparkle of the former more than compensated for the dullness of the latter. About *Miss Grant,* the *Motion Picture Herald* wrote: "It is Miss Ball who carries the picture, which again points her up as one of the most promising light comediennes on the Hollywood scene." The critics' enthusiasm for Lucy saved *Easy Living* from being a total disaster. *Variety* called her role "expertly done," and the *Citizen News* reflected, "Lucille Ball plays that wise-cracking secretary role . . . with one arm tied behind her."

Like moviegoers, Columbia was indeed delighted with *Miss Grant Takes Richmond,* and in February 1950, S. Sylvan Simon began shooting its follow-up, *The Fuller*

Lucy "loosens up."

Touchdown Lucy
on location for *Easy Living*.

B-R.1580A

Lucille Ball, *Easy Living.* 1948.

A. Preparing for air time, "My Favorite Husband" company included Gordon Hughes, Lucy, and Richard Denning. Wilbur Hatch, seated in background, provided the music.

A bird on the head is worth two on a perch, when Bob Hope, posing as Lucy's butler, surprises her with a new coiffure.

Doing it over 'til she gets it right, naive Ellen Grant sharpens her secretarial skills, not realizing her boss is really a bookie in disguise.

Trading her typewriter for a bulldozer, Lucy saves the day for a new housing development and makes an honest man of her boss.

Fancy liar Bob Hope tries to convince Lucy that his English heritage did not include horsemanship in Paramount's *Fancy Pants*.

Lucille Ball, 1949

Did'ja ever have one of those days? Lucille Ball did as *The Fuller Brush Girl.*

Lucille Ball guest-starred on Ed Wynn's early 1949 television series on CBS—and again in 1952 on his NBC "All Star Revue."

Brush Girl, a sequel to his earlier Skelton hit. Red, in fact, made a cameo appearance in this comedy, about a cosmetics salesgirl who stumbles onto a murder and smuggling ring. The film co-starred Eddie Albert as Lucy's long-suffering boyfriend.

"My Favorite Husband" completed its second season in June, with Oppenheimer, Carroll, and Pugh already outlining plans for its return in the fall. CBS, meanwhile, had asked Lucy to consider converting her radio series to television. Since Berle's auspicious debut in 1948, TV had grown by leaps and bounds, and all the net-works had plans to switch their big radio hits to the new medium. Lucy had but one request—that Desi Arnaz be cast as her husband. The network and sponsor balked at the notion, and Lucy and Desi began to think of ways they *could* work together—if not in "My Favorite Husband," then maybe in yet a new television situation comedy all their own.

To prove to themselves, as well as to the CBS brass, that audiences would accept them as a team, the Arnazes toured the country during the summer of 1950 in a music-and-comedy vaudeville act. Desi performed his usual Latin melodies, and Lucy joined him in sketches created by her radio writers. The show was a tremendous success, and when they returned to their home in California, the Arnazes were more convinced than ever that they could make good in a television program together.

Fancy Pants opened in late summer, and, while not repeating the success of *Sorrowful Jones,* was well received by the ticket-buying public. In its review, *Cue* magazine repeated what had become a classic, if not clichéd, compliment: "Lucille Ball is one of the finest comediennes in Hollywood." By the end of September, Co-lumbia had released *The Fuller Brush Girl. Variety* called the film "a rollicking, slam-bang, slapstick comedy with Lucille Ball at her very best." And the *Hollywood Reporter* praised her as "a wide-eyed beauty with buoyant charm" who "puts over her comedy with perfect timing."

Such praise, however, fell on Columbia's deaf ears. S. Sylvan Simon had died suddenly at age forty, after completing *Born Yesterday* with Judy Holliday (in a role Lucy would have loved to have played), and with him went Lucy's only influence at the studio's front office. Holliday was being touted as an Oscar contender (indeed, she

A. Trying to be together as much as possible, Lucy and Desi socialize with old friends (a) at New York's 21 Club with Nancy Walker, and (b) at the Hollywood premiere of *Johnny Belinda* with Eddie Cantor.

B. Aladdin and Ali Baba never had the luck Lucy experienced with *The Magic Carpet,* a 1950 Arabian nights adventure with John Agar.

won that year), and Lucy was suddenly an also-ran comedienne. Harry Cohn, tyrannical head of the studio, credited Simon, not Lucy, with the success of her films, and with him gone, Cohn plotted to cancel Lucy's still unchosen third film.

Cecil B. De Mille, meanwhile, was busy casting his latest Paramount spectacle, *The Greatest Show on Earth*. The film pioneer wanted Lucy to play a prominent role as an elephant trainer; delighted, she naively asked Cohn to postpone production of her next Columbia comedy so she could accept this flattering offer. Always the sly businessman, Cohn denied her request, assigned Lucy to do the worst possible potboiler, and waited blissfully for her to refuse the picture. (He knew Lucy would not miss the opportunity of working with the great De Mille in order to make a grade-C bomb.) He could then, in good conscience, simply fire her and save $85,000.

To his chagrin, Lucy knew exactly what Cohn was up to, called his bluff, and cordially agreed to do his script, a piece of garbage titled *The Magic Carpet* in which she would portray a belly dancer. Her only concern was to get the picture over with in time to join the De Mille picture in January 1951. However, by the time *Carpet* wrapped, Lucy had learned that she was pregnant.

Because of the baby, she would have to bow out of the De Mille movie, but the pregnancy would allow her and Desi to work on plans for their new TV series. They had no way of knowing that it, even more than De Mille's venture, would be worthy of the appellation, "The Greatest Show on Earth."

☆ ☆ ☆ ☆ ☆

Lucille Ball, 1951.

Lucille Ball, Desi Arnaz, "I Love Lucy."

Everybody Loves Lucy

★ ★ ★ ★ ★

Lucy as "The Professor" in nightclub sequence from "I Love Lucy" pilot, March 1951.

"**I** love Lucy and she loves me."

This simple seven-word phrase summed up the premise of the television series developed for Lucille Ball and Desi Arnaz during the spring of 1951. While other TV programs would be built around everything from witches to hillbillies to men from outer space, "I Love Lucy," as the Arnaz show was titled, emphasized and explored basic human emotions. The characters experienced friendship, jealousy, competitiveness, the need to succeed, and, most of all, love.

Jess Oppenheimer, Bob Carroll, and Madelyn Pugh, Lucy's radio writers, went to work on "I Love Lucy" as soon as CBS gave the Arnazes the go-ahead to try a television pilot together. With Lucy pregnant, time was of the essence. For this first effort, Lucy and Desi portrayed themselves—a movie star and a successful orchestra leader. The writers wove their script around the Arnazes' vaudeville act, limiting the action to two basic sets: the stars' living room and a nightclub stage.

In April, the film was sent to New York in search of a sponsor, and Lucy retired to Chatsworth to spend the last three months of her pregnancy in relative peace. A few weeks later, she and Desi received word that CBS had sold their show to

Lucy and Desi, 1951.

Philip Morris cigarettes and that "I Love Lucy" would premiere as a weekly comedy in October.

There followed a minor panic when CBS requested that "Lucy" be produced "live" from New York. Neither of the Arnazes had a desire to leave their cozy California ranch —particularly with a new baby— and Desi, in a fit of desperation, traded away part of his and Lucy's weekly salaries in exchange for the option of doing their show on film in Hollywood. He also wangled all ownership rights to the films after broadcast. Bill Paley, head of the network, considered this a fool-proof deal—he privately predicted the series would fold within six weeks.

Incorporated as Desilu Productions, the new "I Love Lucy" company worked feverishly to make the doomsayers wrong. Oppenheimer, Carroll, and Pugh modified their original story line by changing Desi to Ricky Ricardo, a struggling young band-leader, and by dropping Lucy out of show business entirely. Renamed Lucy Ricardo, she would be a stagestruck, zany housewife who constantly seeks a more glamorous position in life. The locale of the show was moved from California to an upper East Side brownstone at fictional 623 East 68th Street. Bill Frawley was hired to portray the Ricardos' landlord, Fred Mertz, and Vivian Vance, a young stage actress discovered at the La Jolla Playhouse in California, was cast as Fred's frumpish wife Ethel.

On July 17, 1951, Lucy gave

"Call for Philip Morris . . . ?"

DuBarry Was a Lady) were used, each shooting continuously from different angles.

Although Desi's official title read "Executive Producer," Jess Oppenheimer is the one that Lucy called the "Bossman." Indeed, Desi referred to Jess as "the man behind the Ball," because, as producer and head writer for the series, Oppenheimer controlled everything that went into it. Carroll and Pugh actually authored the teleplays, with Oppenheimer editing and polishing the scripts to fit into what he had conceived as the series' formula.

What *was* this formula? What was it that made "I Love Lucy" an immediate hit on its first broad-

birth to her first child, Lucie Desiree Arnaz. Recalling the event a few years later, Lucy commented, "Lucie completely changed the course of my life, as well as Desi's. Children are startling—a miracle. One day there are just two people in the house, and the next day a third person is there, affecting the entire household immediately. Lucie made a different life for us at once . . . and such a wonderful one."

Four weeks after little Lucie's arrival, Desilu took over two sound stages at General Service Studios, where Lucy had worked a few years earlier on the motion picture, *Lured*. They knocked out a wall, built permanent movie-type sets, installed bleachers to seat 300, and hung out a shingle reading "Desilu Playhouse." Within two weeks, the company was ready to start what Lucy called "a three-act play before an audience, filmed like a movie, recorded like radio, and released to television."

The first episode, "Lucy Thinks Ricky Is Trying to Murder Her,"

Lucy's Desilu buddies help celebrate Little Lucie's christening, September 30, 1951: (Left to right) Vivian Vance, Karl Freund, Lucy, camera coordinator Emily Daniels, and director Marc Daniels.

started rehearsals September 3 and went before the cameras September 8. A schedule was established, allowing the cast of "I Love Lucy" to rehearse four or five days on each episode, with the show being filmed on the evening of the final rehearsal day in front of an invited audience. Three cameras, under the direction of Karl Freund (who had first worked with Lucy on

cast, October 15, 1951—and every Monday thereafter? Basically, the series allowed husbands and wives to laugh at the problems in their own marriages. Even little Junior could join in on the fun. The situations rang true—when Lucy Ricardo dived into the world of farce, the viewer went right along with her because the basic situation was believable.

Original opening titles for "I Love Lucy" featured animated Lucy and Ricky figures.

"I LOVE LUCY"

"The Mockingbird Murder Mystery" made impressionable Lucy certain that hubby Ricky was trying to do away with her . . .

In the opening show, for example, Lucy and Ethel bicker with their husbands over how to celebrate the Mertzes' anniversary. The girls insist on going to a nightclub, the boys opting for the fights. When the girls announce they are planning to go out with other men, Ricky and Fred privately decide to forego the fights, to find dates of their own, and to spy on their wives at the club. The fun begins when Ricky and Lucy call the same "matchmaker" for date suggestions. Lucy realizes what the boys are planning and, using her own brand of fiendish wiles, arranges for Ethel and herself to be their husbands' blind dates!

Underlying many subsequent stories was Lucy Ricardo's determination to break into show business. Two early episodes, "The

Diet" and "The Audition," made use of material the Arnazes had performed in their 1950 vaudeville act (and their TV pilot), with Lucy actually appearing—however briefly—with husband Ricky's band.

A favorite plot device used in many early "Lucy" scripts was "the bet," with the girls challenging the boys in order to prove a point. One bet found Lucy and Ethel trying to keep from gossiping about a neighbor, while another had the Ricardos and Mertzes trying to survive a so-called "pioneer" existence.

The pressures of turning out a new show each and every week prompted the writers to borrow ideas from their own earlier work. Some of Lucy Ricardo's cleverest escapades—"The Seance," "Break the Lease," and "Lucy Plays Cupid," among others—were actually rewrites of plots originally used on "My Favorite Husband."

By May 1952, Lucille Ball was considered television's biggest success. The four national rating services then in operation were in unaccustomed agreement: "I Love Lucy" was the nation's number one show. Desilu filmed thirty-eight half-hour episodes that season, but CBS telecast only thirty-five, the remaining three having been set aside to give the company

. . . and Ethel's cards only made her more suspicious.

a head start on the 1952–53 season. A new production obstacle, meanwhile, was developing at home: Lucy had become pregnant again.

When the Arnazes first learned about Lucy's condition, Desi conferred with Bossman Oppenheimer, who came up with the notion that Lucy could have her baby twice—once in real life and again on film as Lucy Ricardo. This never before attempted gimmick would supply the series with human interest, excitement, and —most important—a theme for its second season. It was later decided that because Lucy was planning to have her child by Caesarean section, both the Arnaz baby and the Ricardo baby could be born on the same date.

The pregnancy stories were filmed on a sped-up basis so Lucy

A regular pigpen? "It's not a *regular* one, but it'll do!"

Ragtime Cowboy Lucy.

Academy declared the show to be the Best Comedy Program of the season. A few weeks later, Lucy and Desi signed the biggest television contract written to that date. For about half of the $8 million involved, the Arnazes agreed to continue their weekly "I Love Lucy" telecasts for the next two and a half years.

Petunia Ricardo brushes up her ballet with Madame LaMond (Mary Wickes).

could retire from the show in November; the baby was expected in January. Among the story lines created by the "I Love Lucy" scribes was a touching segment in which Lucy Ricardo seeks just the right moment to tell her husband about her condition—only finally to tell him in the middle of his nightclub act at the Tropicana. Other scripts found Lucy being irritable and temperamental, giving her show-business swan song, becoming a sculptress, hiring an English tutor, and diligently rehearsing her trip to the hospital.

The sex of the Ricardo infant was kept secret until January 19, 1953, when Desi Arnaz IV and Ricky Ricardo, Jr., were both delivered on schedule.

A whopping 71.7 percent of all American television homes watched the arrival of Little Ricky that night, but the viewing public were not the only ones who had fallen head over heels in love with Lucy. On February 5, the Academy of Television Arts and Sciences selected her as Comedienne of the Year, 1952. The entire "I Love Lucy" staff was honored when the

Lucy stayed home two full months after her son's birth, caring for the child as proudly and dutifully as any mother. Meanwhile, her TV program continued to appear on CBS every Monday night through the use of shows which had been filmed before the baby was born and by rerunning old episodes using the flashback technique. In all of these programs, the viewers were constantly reminded of the new Ricardo baby.

"I Love Lucy" resumed production in March on the first of eleven episodes that would finish off the series' second season. Once filming was completed in May, Lucy and Desi trooped over to MGM to begin work on their first motion picture together in thirteen years, *The Long, Long Trailer.* The rest of the Desilu company pulled up roots at General Services and moved to more spacious quarters at nearby Motion Picture Center.

The third season of Ricardo misadventures started on October 5, with the comedy leaning heavily toward the old slapstick routines that had made the show such a success in 1951. In one segment, for example, Lucy went through a commercial laundry's washing and starching machines to retrieve half of a lucky dollar bill. This was also the year that Tennessee Ernie Ford made two guest appearances

"Ethel to Tillie . . . Ethel to Tillie . . ."

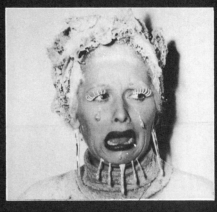

Tired of high-priced beef? Lucy's got
"sirloin, tenderloin, T-bone, rump, pot roast,
chuck roast, oxtail, stump."

"All right, Ethel, let's have those biscuits!"

"Ricky Ricardo isn't appearing here anymore?"

She could always dye it black and become a Smith Brother.

A. We're having a baby . . .

B. Lucy charlestons with (left to right) Gertrude Astor, Helen Dixon, Hazel Pierce, and Barbara Pepper. Barbara, an old pal from Lucille Ball's Goldwyn days, appeared in nearly a dozen "Lucy" shows over the years.

C. A living doll . . . Lucy gets trapped in a fur salon.

HENDERSON'S FURS

on the show as a country bumpkin house guest. In the first program, he tried to sleep on the Mertzes' rollaway bed the hard way—without opening it. The shows, however, were not all clowning and games. Many of the episodes ended with a tender kiss-and-make-up scene. In one memorable sequence, the Ricardos celebrated their wedding anniversary in the living room closet in order to be alone for the occasion.

Desilu filmed the one-hundredth episode of "I Love Lucy" on June 17, 1954, the celebration accompanied by an apprehension that something new would have to be injected into the series come fall. Over the summer, Oppenheimer, Carroll, and Pugh came up with the idea of taking the Ricardos and Mertzes to Hollywood, with Ricky getting a movie offer.

Like the carefully laid baby plans, the California trip proved to be a stroke of genius. Starting with the telecast of November 8, the writers based scripts around everything from Ricky taking a screen test to Lucy learning how to drive. Three stories documented the Ricardos' and Mertzes' cross-country auto trip, one reuniting the foursome with "cuzzin" Ernie Ford in Bent Fork, Tennessee.

Once Lucy Ricardo arrived in California, there was no limit to her mischievousness. For the first time, "I Love Lucy" could make legitimate use of guest stars playing themselves, and between February and May 1955, some of Hollywood's biggest names visited the show. In one sequence, Eve Arden and William Holden had the misfortune of meeting Lucy at the Brown Derby restaurant where Holden wound up literally wearing his lunch. Perhaps the highlight of the season occurred on the program of May 9, guest-starring Harpo Marx. The Silent One and the Redhead (impersonating Marx) performed face to face on opposite sides of a room partition. The routine remains today as one of Lucy's best.

Despite the new locale and big name guests, the basic "I Love Lucy" format never changed. Glamorous Hollywood only whetted Lucy Ricardo's wacky ways. During her visit to the movie capital, she romped over such sacred ground as the MGM studios, where she forced her way into the movies; Richard Widmark's Beverly Hills home, where she picked a grapefruit; the Don Loper salon, where she modeled a wool suit while

sporting a severe sunburn; and the previously mentioned Brown Derby.

While fictional Lucy and Ricky Ricardo cavorted around Hollywood, Lucy and Desi Arnaz were likewise making news in the film capital. In the spring of 1955 they purchased controlling interest in Motion Picture Center, and in the summer they used the studio to house their latest feature film effort, *Forever Darling,* to be released through MGM.

On October 3, "I Love Lucy" launched its fifth year, with Proctor and Gamble and General Foods now sponsoring the show. Two new writers, Bob Schiller and Bob Weiskopf, had joined the series, and the new fall scripts would take Lucy from California to New York and then on to Europe.

Recalling Lucy's expressed hopes to be able to retire "while on top" once her series contracts expired in June, Jess Oppenheimer wanted 1955–56 to be "I Love Lucy's" best year. With his writing team of four, Jess drew up an outline for seventeen teleplays to be included in the new European serial. The first three stories took place at home and concerned preparations for the trip. Two more chronicled Lucy's adventures aboard the steamship *Constitution.* The remaining twelve shows, telecast between February and May, took place overseas, with the Ricardos and Mertzes visiting the United Kingdom, France, Switzerland, Italy, and Monaco.

During the course of the trip, Lucy dangled from a helicopter, wedged herself into a ship's porthole, faked a fox hunt on a posh English estate, modeled a Paris gunnysack original, got caught in an avalanche, and, in a dream sequence, was nearly eaten alive by a Scottish dragon.

On the way to Rome, Lucy landed a role in an Italian movie, *Bitter Grapes.* Thinking the film to be about the wine industry, she visited a local vineyard, where grapes were still being pressed by hand—or, should one say, by foot. The resulting chaos, with Lucy first squashing around in the vat of grapes, then being harassed into an all-out grape fight with one of the workers, made this episode one of the most popular "I Love Lucy" segments of all time.

"Homeward Bound," telecast May 14, 1956, found the Redhead smuggling an overweight piece of cheese on board the plane home.

D. Lucy and the furnace pipe—the "snooper's friend."

E. Lucille Ball would do *anything* for a laugh, as was evidenced by this classic episode set in a candy factory. Desi helps her clean up.

F. . . . my baby and me.

137

Disguised first as a baby, the cheese was later cut into small portions and methodically stuffed into Ricky's band instruments. The program ended on a happy—if not melodic—note, with the troupe arriving once again in New York. It was episode 153 of the series, the last first-run show of the season, and the final installment to be produced and/or written by Jess Oppenheimer, who had resigned to join NBC as an executive.

With Desi Jr. now three years old and Little Lucie approaching five, Mama Lucy was interested in cutting back her career activities in order to be home more with the children. Papa Desi asked CBS to expand the series to an hour and reduce its frequency from once a week to once monthly, but the network flatly refused. Thus, on May 23, CBS and Desilu announced that "I Love Lucy" would return for the full 1956–57 season.

The perennial challenge of creating story ideas for "Lucy" again confronted Carroll, Pugh, Schiller, and Weiskopf during early summer 1956. After the usual experimenting with script possibilities, the quartet decided that the time was right for the Little Ricky character to come of age. When the series returned to CBS in the fall, child actor Keith Thibodeaux (aka Richard Keith) was installed as a permanent cast member portraying the Ricardo son. For the first time since his birth, the character would become an integral figure in the program's weekly story lines, and the Ricardos became a family in every sense of the term. At no time, however, were Lucy's shenanigans ever presented in a vein detrimental to her role as a mother. Likewise, Ricky maintained the dignity and warmth of a responsible father. Keith's extraordinary musical

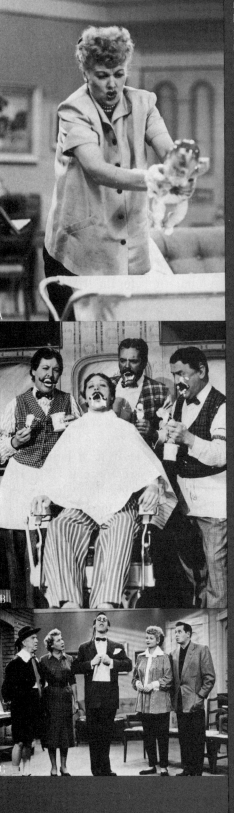

A. Selecting a "unique and euphonious" name was only one of Lucy's problems as she prepared for Baby Ricardo.

B. A close shave, Lucy hits everything but the right notes.

C. "As I tippy tippy toe through my garden . . ."

138

A. Sam and Pete of the *New York Herald Times Tribune* pay a surprise visit to Ricky's daddy shower.

B. Lucy makes a bust of herself.

C. The calm before the storm; Ricky and the Mertzes prepare to take Lucy to the hospital.

D. "Little Ricky is a children," played in 1952 by Richard Lee and Ronald Lee Simmons.

ability made it possible for him to perform father-and-son arrangements with Desi.

On October 1, "I Love Lucy" launched its sixth season with the show's main characters again residing in New York. Locale, however, would no longer be limited to the Mertz apartment building. One of the changes devised by Desilu to keep the show fresh found Ricky Ricardo buying an interest in the Tropicana and renaming it Club Babalu. Bob Hope and Orson Welles guest-starred in the season's opening shows as headliners appearing at the club. The Hope program required an elaborate mock-up of the grandstands at Yankee Stadium, while the Welles show took Lucy and Ethel to Macy's department store. A subsequent episode provided local color via location shooting aboard the Lexington Avenue IRT subway.

A thread of continuity was woven into the early autumn episodes as the Ricardos took a third long-distance trip, this time to Florida to do some fishing. The final episode of this four-part serial found the Ricardos flying to Havana for a short visit with Ricky's relatives. During the thirty-minute escapade, Lucy not only insulted an all-important uncle, but managed to invade his favorite cigar store where she created her own Cuban crisis.

In December, Desilu prepared an "I Love Lucy Christmas Special," for telecast Christmas Eve. The show included a current story (with Fred buying Little Ricky a Christmas tree) and flashbacks as the gang reminisced about their previous adventures.

By February, the Mertz apartment building had been written out of the show, with the Ricardos and Mertzes moving full force out to the suburbs of Connecticut. Two new neighbors, Ralph and Betty

"One more hour and they'd have reported the death of another salesman."

A. Redheaded rock meets immovable force, Mrs. Porter (Verna Felton).

B. Lucy wins an Emmy, February 5, 1953.

Ramsey, were added to the cast, portrayed by Frank Nelson and Mary Jane Croft.

Lucy in Connecticut, like Lucy anyplace else, was as irrepressible as ever. In one program, she planned an evening in Manhattan for the group—only to discover that her theatre tickets were for the matinee performance. Another sequence found Lucy and Ethel dismantling a freshly built barbecue in search of Lucy's lost wedding ring. The Redhead and Betty Ramsey vied for first place in a flower contest, both contestants unknowingly entering wax tulips, both being disqualified as their beautiful specimens melted in the hot summer sun.

"The Ricardos Dedicate a Statue," the final first-run episode of the season, was telecast Monday evening, May 6. Viewers who had been keeping up with the TV logs knew that this—"I Love Lucy"'s 180th production—would be the series' last. Desi had finally convinced CBS to let his company convert the show to occasional one-hour specials, allowing Lucy more time with her children and Desi himself more time with Desilu's quickly growing business empire. At the time, no one could

A cast for all seasons . . . Viv, Bill, Desi, and whatshername . . . ?

have predicted that "I Love Lucy" would continue to entertain millions of viewers throughout the world in countless reruns, earning ratings and public acceptance equal to and often better than new first-run programs. "I Love Lucy" retired in May 1957, but it would live on forever.

The adventures of Lucy and Ricky Ricardo were continued on CBS during the following three seasons with a series of thirteen hour-long "Lucille Ball-Desi Arnaz Show" specials. The first (which actually ran seventy-five rather than sixty minutes) told how Lucy MacGillicuddy met and married her Cuban conga-drum-mer. Other shows found Tallulah Bankhead moving in next door and Danny Thomas renting out the Ricardos' Connecticut home. Many of the shows found the principals traveling, and in the course of the three years, they visited Sun Valley, Alaska, Mexico, Japan, and Las Vegas.

"Lucy Wins a Race Horse," which, along with the Danny Thomas episode, ranks as the best of the specials, included one of the most memorable "Lucy" scenes of all time: Lucy and Ethel coaxing a horse up the living room stairs, hoping to hide the steed from a disapproving Ricky. Later in the hour, Lucy dons her jockey togs and actually races the horse in a local sulky contest.

Most of the specials, however, added little to the now established "Lucy legend." They sustained, rather than enhanced, America's love affair with the adorable Redhead. By the spring of 1960, Lucy and Desi realized it was time to quit. Although their own marriage was also coming apart, their decision to end the Ricardo-Mertz escapades was based on creative rather than personal considerations. Hence, they walked away and left for posterity perhaps the greatest, most consistently first-rate comedy series ever created for television.

Philip Morris made the Arnazes the highest-paid stars on television.

Another fine mess . . .

143

"It's a moo-moo."

Lucy humors her mother's friend's roommate's cousin's middle boy . . .

"The first hundred are the hardest." Lucy and Desi cut the cake celebrating the completion of their one hundredth episode.

With Lucy behind the wheel, traffic was backed up all the way to East Orange, New Jersey

Lucy schemed to get around Teensy and Weensy (which was no short trip) . . .

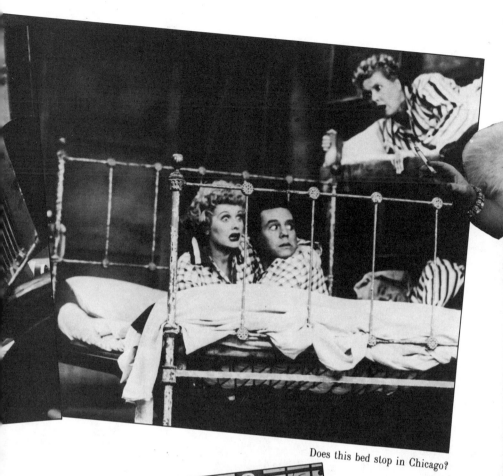

Does this bed stop in Chicago?

They may be people, but they're not like
you and me . . .

Flaming redhead . . .

A. Lucy gets ahead in pictures.

B. "Honestly, Ethel, if you're going to get cold feet on a routine souvenir hunt . . . !"

C. "Well, I didn't do it by draggin' my foot."

Desi's first birthday.

The Arnazes joined the 1953 Santa Claus Lane Parade in Hollywood.

Lucille Ball and Vivian Vance . . . wacky, warm, and wonderful.

Tallyho!

"But, waiter, this food has snails in it!"

Lucy spends a bewitching evening in Little Ricky's school pageant.

Junior joins the act.

It's a bird, it's a plane, it's Lucy.

Lucy soaks up local color.

"Gee, Lucy, look—it isn't flat anymore!"

"He doesn't want us to come to dinner . . . he wants us to *be* dinner!"

Lucy's parting shot.

Lucy tells the bull where to get off.

Everywhere a chick, chick . . .

Lucy has a horse guest.

Lucy and Desi appeared as the Ricardos for the last time in "Lucy Meets the Moustache," telecast April 1, 1960.

Together again, Lucy and Red cavort in a Freddie the Freeloader sketch in "Lucy Goes to Alaska."

★★★★★ Starring Lucille Ball

"I Love Lucy" accomplished in a mere fifteen months what Lucille Ball had been striving to achieve for over eighteen years: it made Lucy a household name, a star by every definition. By the time Little Ricky/Desi IV were born on January 19, 1953, the Arnazes were television's most popular performers, and their popularity made them prime candidates for lucrative motion picture offers.

As early as May 1952, Desi became interested in acquiring film rights to the Clinton Twiss novel about life in a motor home, *The Long, Long Trailer*. To his chagrin, MGM outbid him. MGM, in this instance, was producer Pandro S. Berman, one of Lucy's old RKO cohorts, who agreed with Desi that the Arnazes should star in the property. The other studio brass, however, had reservations. "Metro," Berman later recalled, "wanted no part of it. They subscribed to the theory that the audience wouldn't pay to see actors they could get at home for free. But I insisted these were different parts, and Lucille Ball and Desi Arnaz could make the picture hilarious. If the picture was funny enough, I had no worries that enough people wouldn't pay to see it."

On February 4, 1953, just two weeks after Lucy's babies arrived, *Variety*

Lucille Ball, 1952.

164

announced that Lucy and Desi had been engaged by MGM at a whopping $250,000 combined salary to star in the film. A week later, noted director Vincente Minnelli joined the project.

"I Love Lucy" completed production for the 1952–53 season on May 29, and after a quick one-week vacation, Lucy and Desi started work on *The Long, Long Trailer.* Unlike the TV series, *Trailer*

☆ ☆ ☆ ☆ ☆ ☆ ☆ ☆ ☆ ☆
☆ ☆ ☆ ☆ ☆ ☆ ☆ ☆ ☆ ☆
☆ ☆ ☆ ☆ ☆ ☆ ☆ ☆ ☆ ☆

A. Money, Money, Money . . . Lucy and Desi are dismayed to learn that their old car is not powerful enough to pull the trailer they have just bought from Herb Vigran.

B. Carrying the bride across the threshold, Desi gets ample assistance from nosy Marjorie Main, who thinks Lucy has sprained her ankle.

would be filmed in color, with beautiful location shooting at Yosemite National Park.

The script, adapted from the Twiss novel by Albert Hackett and Frances Goodrich *(Father of the Bride, Easter Parade),* concerned a newlywed couple who think they can enjoy life criss-crossing the country in a house trailer. There were no major supporting roles, so

MGM peopled the cast with such notable character actors as Herb Vigran, Marjorie Main, Ida Moore, Madge Blake, and Peter Leeds. Lucy's old MGM co-star, Keenan Wynn, appeared in a cameo role as a disgruntled traffic cop.

Vincente Minnelli, in his memoirs, recalled the production as a very happy experience: "On that picture we were all lovely and tal-

ented and well-mannered. . . . All film-making should be as easy. . . . There were times when the action was broad, and those were the opportunities Lucy grabbed hold of and ran away with. . . . Lucy is one of the few comedic talents who can be broad and uniquely human at the same time."

Production ended July 16, with the Arnazes spending the balance

A. No Joy Ride: Lucy discovers that cooking and driving don't mix when she tries to prepare an evening meal before Desi stops for the night.

B. Twenty years away from Oscar-dom, seven-year-old Liza Minnelli visited Lucy on the set of her daddy's production of *The Long, Long Trailer.*

of their summer resting in Del Mar, California, a seaside resort town near San Diego. September 8 started another season's worth of "I Love Lucy" episodes, but by this time Desilu had managed to whittle down the production schedule to four days per week. Rehearsals typically began on Monday, with filming set for Thursday evenings. In February, however, two episodes had to be produced virtually back to back, one on Thursday, another on the following Tuesday, in order to enable the Arnazes to be in New York for the opening of *The Long, Long Trailer.*

If the Arnazes had any doubts about their own popularity, this trip dispelled them. As one magazine later reported, "When Lucy and Desi went to lunch, it took ten cops to get them through the crowds."

The pair arrived in New York on Thursday, February 18, to face a staggering schedule of personal appearances. *Trailer* was to be the keystone of MGM's Thirtieth Anniversary Jubilee, and the studio was sparing no coin in the publicity department. Upon arrival, Lucy met and posed for newsreel reporters and photographers. Then came

a trip through Times Square in a trailer (like the one used in the movie) with Desi driving, followed by appearances for the Heart Fund, interviews, a second charity gathering, a press party for 400 people at the Waldorf-Astoria Hotel, dinner at the penthouse of Radio City Music Hall—where *Trailer* was premiering—and an appearance onstage at the theatre following the movie. That was only day one. This whirlwind schedule continued for ten days.

When the reviews came out, Lucy found herself with her first hit movie in five years. *Time* magazine called it "a wonderfully slap-happy farce," and *Newsweek, Commonwealth,* and *American Magazine* all found it "hilarious." So did the ticket-buying public: When the receipts were counted, *The Long, Long Trailer* had replaced *Father of the Bride* as the top grossing MGM comedy up to that time.

Trailer was also the first motion picture to star personalities who had become "hot box office attractions" as a result of their televi-

sion exposure. While the big movie studios still viewed the new medium with contempt, *Trailer*'s success prompted them also to see television as a source for new material. Later in 1954, for instance, Warner Bros. released a feature version of *Dragnet,* and in 1955, the same studio issued a film based on *Our Miss Brooks.*

MGM, meanwhile, was anxious to duplicate the success of *The Long, Long Trailer* with another Lucy-Desi movie. The property everyone agreed upon was *Forever, Darling,* a comedy concerning a research scientist, his wacky wife, and the guardian angel who saves their marriage. The Arnazes, of course, would play the couple, and James Mason was cast as the visiting angel. Louis Calhern, John Emery, John Hoyt, Natalie Schafer, Mabel Albertson, and Nancy Kulp also appeared.

Unlike *Trailer, Forever, Darling* was produced by Desi Arnaz (as Zanra Productions) at his TV studio, with many members of the "I Love Lucy" crew duplicating their chores for the film. MGM financed and would distribute the finished picture. Alexander Hall, an old friend of Lucy's who had directed over a dozen of Columbia's greatest

A flustered Desi "prunes" Aunt Anastasia's prize rose bush with his two-and-a-half-ton, twenty-eight-foot "monster."

Still a showgirl at heart, Lucy kicks
up her heels with the Rockettes
backstage at Radio City Music Hall.

comedies, directed from a script by
Helen Deutsch. With location
shooting again taking place in Yosemite National Park, *Forever,
Darling* had a seven-week production schedule, May 31 through
July 14, 1955.

Metro slotted *Forever, Darling*
for late-winter release, premiering
the film February 9, 1956, at New
York's Loew's State Theatre. Again
the Arnazes went east for the occasion, this time stopping off at
Lucy's hometown of Celeron/
Jamestown for an old-fashioned
reunion. However, public and crit-

ical response to this film was limited. *Newsweek*, for instance,
called it "silly," and *Time* deemed
it a "garbled story" in which "not
until the final reel does Lucy get
around to taking the pratfalls that
are her television specialty."

Pratfalls were not the only missing ingredient—so were the everyday, common-man touches that
had made "My Favorite Husband,"
"I Love Lucy," and *The Long, Long
Trailer* so appealing. America
loved the Ricardos because they
were just like the folks next door—
only funnier. Audiences had little

sympathy for *Darling*'s upper-
class family, and, although the
fantasy motif with Mason was en-
joyable, it seemed overly con-
trived. In the final analysis, only
the Arnazes' most loyal fans truly
loved this new Lucy.

The failure of the picture convinced Lucille Ball that she should
stay close to what her television
public had come to expect: everyday situations exaggerated into
slapstick comedy. Within a year,
however, it was time to call it quits
with "I Love Lucy," and the
"Lucy-Desi" specials were created.

Nothing is more important to Lucy than her appearance . . .

With the money received from selling their series reruns to CBS, the Arnazes purchased the real estate owned by their old alma mater, RKO, and turned it into Desilu Studios. Desi started a weekly dramatic anthology, "Desilu Playhouse," on CBS, and Lucy agreed to appear each week in the "wraparounds," introducing the following week's show.

On November 17, 1958, Lucy stepped into the "Playhouse" spotlight as "K.O. Kitty," a dancing teacher who inherits an uncoordinated prizefighter. The show, directed by Jerry Thorpe, was written by Lucy's favorite scribes, Bob Carroll and Madelyn Pugh, who, incidentally, had recently married "Playhouse" producer Quinn Martin.

Danny Thomas, Ann Sothern, and Milton Berle all guest-starred on individual "Lucy-Desi" specials, and to return the favor, the Arnazes appeared on their respective programs—portraying Lucy and Ricky Ricardo. "The Danny Thomas Show" of January 5, 1959, for example, found the Ricardos houseguesting with the Danny Williams family. Ricky hoped that Mrs. Williams's conservative manners might rub off on Lucy, but, of course, just the opposite proved true. This was the Ricardos' first adventure without the familiar Mertzes.

Lucy went it totally alone—without even Ricky—on "The Ann Sothern Show" of October 5, 1959, in which she checked into New

York's fictional Bartley House hotel to visit Katy O'Connor (Ann), her "old friend and school chum." A month later, on November 1, the Ricardos visited Las Vegas for a "Milton Berle Show" on NBC. The story line had Ricky and Berle entertaining at the same hotel and Lucy trying to patch up a spat between Miltie and his wife, Ruth.

None of these projects excited Lucille Ball as much as the "Desilu Workshop," a little theatre group she had started to give new television talent a chance to learn the craft. Some 1,700 aspiring young professionals had been tested, and twenty-one winners received Workshop contracts. The old RKO Studio Club had been remodeled into a 180-seat theatre to house the repertory group. Hence, much of the guidance that Lucy had once received from Lela Rogers, Ginger's mother, was being passed on to others.

By the fall of 1959, the Arnaz

marriage was beyond repair, and Lucy began toying with the idea of moving to New York to do a Broadway play. In March of 1960, with divorce proceedings pending, Lucy purchased stage rights to N. Richard Nash's script for a new "comedy with music" entitled *Wildcat.*

With the musical not scheduled to start rehearsals until early autumn, Lucy agreed to co-star with Bob Hope in a new motion picture, *The Facts of Life.* To be filmed in part on the old "I Love Lucy" sound stage at Desilu, the movie was written by its producer, Norman Panama, and its director, Melvin Frank, who had been kicking around the idea for the picture since 1953. Featured in supporting roles would be Ruth Hussey, Don DeFore, and Louis Nye.

The rather adult (for 1960) story line can best be summed up by one of Lucy's own voice-over soliloquies: "Am I really doing this? Me? Kitty Webster, Pasadena housewife, secretary of the PTA, den mother of the Cub Scouts? . . . Have I really come to Monterey to spend a weekend with the husband of my best friend?"

Production commenced on *The Facts of Life* on June 2, almost one full month after Lucy had filed for a divorce. Filming was delayed, however, when, on July 1, she fell and was knocked unconscious while performing for the cameras. An ambulance rushed her to nearby Cedars of Lebanon Hospi-

tal, where she was treated for severe facial and leg bruises. She returned to *The Facts of Life* a few days later, the picture was completed in August, and United Artists booked the comedy for Christmas release.

Wildcat opened to a capacity house at New York's Alvin Theatre

. . . unless it is getting a laugh.

on December 16, 1960. The little girl who had run away from home more than once to be on the Broadway stage had finally made it—after more than thirty years! Some of the critics disliked the book, others the music, still others found fault with the male chorus line —but they were unanimous in their praise of Lucy. For days after the opening, the box office was swamped by crowds wanting to order tickets to see their favorite redhead.

For the first time in many years, Lucy was appearing in a role other than Lucy Ricardo. She was now Wildcat Jackson, a tomboyish oil prospector seeking her fortune in

the turn-of-the-century West. The cast included Keith Andes as drillteam boss Joe Dynamite; Paula Stewart as Wildcat's sister, Janie; Dan Tomkins as Sookie, a mischievous old prospector; and Edith King as Countess Emily O'Brien. The show was directed and choreographed by Michael Kidd, co-pro-

Forever, Darling, a comedy originally conceived in the mid-forties for Lucy and William Powell, was based on the short story by Marya Mannes, "The Woman Who Was Scared."

duced by N. Richard Nash. Thirteen lively production numbers were supplied by Cy Coleman and Carolyn Leigh.

The Facts of Life opened in late December to applause from the public and critics alike. *Time* magazine, for example, loved the film, calling it "the funniest U. S. film since *The Apartment.*" Before long, Hope's staff quietly started scouting for yet another movie property to star Bob and Lucy.

Miss Ball's ambitions that winter were unfortunately not equalled by her physical condition. In February, she was forced to leave *Wildcat* for two weeks because of fatigue and a serious cold, and she later fractured a finger and injured her back. In May, she

A. Lucy, Desi, James Mason (standing), and Louis Calhern headed the cast of *Forever, Darling,* the first and only film produced by Zanra Productions (Arnaz spelled backwards).

fainted on stage during a performance and finally, in June, under doctor's orders, had to leave the show entirely.

After spending the summer in Europe with her two children, Lucy returned to New York in September to complete some unfinished business with a certain nightclub comedian she had met on a blind date the previous winter. On November 18, 1961, Lucy became Mrs. Gary Morton (real name: Morton Goldapper) in a private ceremony performed at the Marble Collegiate Church by the Reverend Dr. Norman Vincent Peale.

A week later, Lucy started rehearsals for a ninety-minute TV special, Leland Hayward's production of *The Good Years.* Based on a book by Walter Lord, the spectacular was scheduled to air on CBS January 12, with Henry Fonda and

Friends since their Goldwyn days, Lucy and Ann Sothern exchanged guest appearances on each other's programs in the late 1950s.

Lucille Ball, 1956.

Lucy and Desi bring crosstown traffic to a standstill as they greet thousands of fans in Manhattan's Times Square.

Mort Sahl co-starring. Included were views of American life from 1900–1914, using songs, dances, and comedy skits. A highlight was Lucy's reenactment of the 1912 Grace Williams trial, wherein a woman was tried for having sung "Everybody's Doin' It" and danced the turkey trot in public. The overall program, however, proved to be an uneven hodgepodge, and in reviewing it for *TV Guide*, columnist Henry Harding noted, "Seldom has so much talent been effectively squandered."

By Christmas 1961, Lucy had discovered two properties which she felt would make movie hits. The first, *Critic's Choice*, would reunite her for the fourth time with Bob Hope. The other, tentatively titled *The Beardsley Story*, would be Desilu's first feature production, with a screenplay prepared by Bob Carroll and Madelyn Pugh Martin.

Desi, meanwhile, was having problems keeping Desilu's television operations solvent. Without question it was time to call home the first string—Lucille Ball and Vivian Vance—and team them in an all new series. In March, a few days before Lucy checked in at Warner Bros. to begin *Critic's Choice*, CBS announced that the comedienne had signed to return to weekly television in a brand new situation comedy that would premiere on the network in October. Sold without pilot or script outline, the series would be developed — of course —by Bob and Madelyn. *The Beardsley Story*, by consequence, would be postponed indefinitely.

Critic's Choice, directed by Don Weis, featured the supporting talents of Marilyn Maxwell, Rip Torn, Jessie Royce Landis, Marie Windsor, and John Dehner. Lucy played a novice playwright who outshines her drama-critic husband (Bob

Now divorced, Lucy and gray-haired Desi were reunited briefly at a studio luncheon kicking off production of *The Facts of Life*, Lucy's third feature with Bob Hope.

One good boost deserves another. Lucy clowns with two of her Desilu Workshops students, Jerry Antes (right) and Dick Kallman. Kallman later starred in the NBC comedy series, "Hank."

Are you sure Romeo and Juliet started this way? An unexpected rainstorm puts the damper on Lucy and Bob's romantic weekend.

Happy Birthday, Lucy: The redhead celebrates her forty-ninth birthday on the set of *The Facts of Life.* Sharing her cake are Bob Hope, director Melvin Frank, and columnist Walter Winchell.

A. "What Takes My Fancy," a *Wildcat* production number (featuring Dan Tomkins), never failed to stop the show.

B. Lucy took time off from her busy *Wildcat* schedule to visit "The Garry Moore Show," which featured the "goofs" and "out-takes" from *The Facts of Life.*

Hope). Unfortunately, no one in the cast could overcome the tired and predictable script, based on the Jean Kerr play. Released in April 1963, the film promptly died at the box office and remains today as one of Lucy and Hope's *least* favorite films.

In November 1962, Lucy replaced the retiring Desi Arnaz as president of Desilu Studios, and suddenly there was little time for motion picture work. *A Guide for the Married Man,* directed by Gene Kelly, allowed her the opportunity to return to the screen in a small, yet wonderful role. An adult comedy, in which Robert Morse tries to teach Walter Matthau how to be a philandering husband, *Guide* included eighteen big-name guest stars who acted out Morse's fantasies. Lucy and Art Carney were teamed as a happily married couple—with Carney being a husband who likes to fool around a little. To get out of the house, he picks a fight with Lucy over her cooking, storms out, has his fling, then phones Lucy the next day to apologize for being quarrelsome. The film, released in the spring of 1967, was a winner on all counts. Lucy and Carney's vignette, in particular, was praised by the critics.

By February 1967, Lucy had grown weary of her chores as studio president and agreed to sell Desilu to Gulf and Western, a giant conglomerate that had recently acquired Paramount Pictures.

The Beardsley Story, retitled *The Population Explosion,* retitled *His, Hers and Theirs,* retitled *Yours, Mine and Ours,* finally went before the cameras on July 5, 1967, with Mel Shavelson directing. Henry Fonda, Van Johnson, Tom Bosley, and eighteen youngsters co-starred. The plot, based on a real-life situation, told the story of a

Lucille Ball, Bob Hope, *Critic's Choice*.

widow, Lucy, with eight children who marries a widower, Fonda, with ten. A warm, happy "family" picture, *Yours, Mine and Ours* included only one "Lucy" scene, but it turned out to be the most memorable moment of the film. It occurs when Lucy, unwittingly drunk, dumps mashed potatoes and milk into the lap of one of Fonda's daughters, then breaks out into a hysterical laughing-and-crying jag.

To promote the film, Lucy and the eighteen kids were guests on the "Ed Sullivan Show" of March 17, 1968. The picture's theme song, by Fred Karlin, was worked into a production number in which Lucy tucked all the youngsters into bed. The feature opened that week—as a major Easter attraction —and proceeded to become one of the highest-grossing films of the year.

Lucy's greatest success in the sixties, however, was not in the movies, but on television. Nothing could compare with her antics in the half-hour situation comedy, "The Lucy Show," particularly when she was clowning with her best buddy, Vivian Vance.

Lucy and Art Carney were in good company in *A Guide for the Married Man*. Also making cameo appearances were Jack Benny, Polly Bergen, Joey Bishop, Sid Caesar, Phil Silvers, and Jayne Mansfield.

I do, he does, they will!

Down the hatch! Lucy doesn't realize that each of Fonda's kids has independently added a little something extra to her drink.

Mr. and Mrs. Gary Morton, 1961.

Lucille Ball, 1968.

HHT-40

★ The New Same Old Lucy Show Rides Again

Lucy wins again! Lucy receives her fourth Emmy Award in sixteen years, May 19, 1968.

*L*ucille Ball began work in the spring of 1962 on her second TV situation comedy, "The Lucy Show," with all the zest, vitality, and anticipation of a ten-year-old child with a new toy. It had been five years since she had last endured the weekly series grind. To assure smooth sailing, Desi Arnaz, as president of Desilu and Lucy's closest business advisor, had reassembled much of the old staff for her, most importantly Vivian Vance and four of the "I Love Lucy" writers (Bob Carroll, Madelyn Martin, Bob Schiller, and Bob Weiskopf).

Veteran nightclub comedian Dick Martin, of Rowan and Martin fame, was signed to guest-star in ten episodes as Lucy's airline pilot neighbor, Harry; Jimmy Garrett and Candy Moore were inked to portray Lucy's children; and Ralph Hart won the role of Sherman, Vivian's son. Elliot Lewis was hired to produce the series, and Jack Donohue, Lucy's old friend from her MGM days, would direct.

"The Lucy Show" concept was, in essence, survival in modern times. Lucy and Viv were cast as two women—Lucy Carmichael, widow, and Vivian Bagley, divorcée—trying to handle the normally masculine details of running a home and, at

Lucille Ball.

"The Lucy Show" cast: Lucille Ball, Vivian Vance, and (standing) Candy Moore, Jimmy Garrett, and Ralph Hart.

Lucy and Viv's new adventures were based loosely on *Life Without George*, a novel by Irene Kampen.

Lucy discovered that returning to television had its ups and downs.

Mr. Barnsdahl, president of the local Danfield, New York, bank and, as such, executor of Lucy's late husband's will. It was he who had to suffer the slings and arrows of Lucy's countless pleas for more money.

"The Lucy Show" was one of the funniest programs on the air during 1962–63, never dropping out of the Top Ten. It was also among the most perilous to produce. Lucy had always agreed to do almost anything for a laugh, and more than once that season she put her physical well-being in jeopardy. In "Lucy Builds a Rumpus Room," for example, a ton of coal fell all around Lucy and Viv. For protection, the girls sported quilted suits, which nevertheless offered no protection for their faces.

In "Lucy and Her Electric Mattress," Lucy worked on stilts, and for "Lucy and Viv Install a Shower," the girls were required to perform onstage in a tank brimming with water. Lucy rode a horse

the same time, attempting to retain enough femininity to attract male companionship. The characters, of course, were not far removed from those created for "I Love Lucy"; only the names and marital status were different.

For the premiere episode, "Lucy Waits Up for Chris," the writers created a "Lucy Show" classic, climaxed by Miss Ball bouncing from a backyard trampoline in through her second-story bedroom window, all the while hiding from her teenaged daughter downstairs. Subsequent scripts found Lucy and Viv breaking into the local YMCA; fencing; buying a sheep (to help keep the grass short); and romping around in a kangaroo suit.

Just as Lucy Ricardo had the Wednesday Afternoon Fine Arts League women's club, Lucy Carmichael started a Women's Volunteer Fire Department, a zany bunch of ladies who banded together to protect the neighborhood but also found time for teas, socials, a barbershop quartet, and a newspaper drive.

One of the lady firefighters was Lucy's friend, actress Mary Wickes. Another was Mary Jane Croft, the gal who had portrayed Betty Ramsey during the last season of "I Love Lucy." (She was also the wife of producer Elliot Lewis.) Character actor Charles Lane, a frequent "I Love Lucy" player, also joined the new show as

in "Lucy Visits the White House" and was actually thrown by her mount during rehearsals. In "Lucy and the Little League," Lucy was accidentally slapped in the eye with a banana peel.

When story conferences for "The Lucy Show" second season were initiated, it was agreed that physical comedy should be deemphasized, with the humor stemming more from verbal hijinks. But for that, Lucy would need a straight man—and to the writers' delight, the best character actor in the business was available: king of the slow burn, Gale Gordon.

Ever since Gale's successful tour of duty as bank president Rudolph Atterbury in "My Favorite

Putting Little Ricky to sleep was never like this!

Husband," Lucy's writers had wanted to reunite the bombastic Gordon with the scatterbrained Ball.

In the new story line, Gordon would again portray a bank president, Theodore J. Mooney. Like his predecessor Barnsdahl (Charles Lane), Mooney would be chief executor of Lucy's trust fund. To get things off to a riotous start, Carroll and Martin dreamed up a two-part story in which Lucy inadvertently locks herself and Mooney in the bank's security vault.

A new policy being introduced on "The Lucy Show" for 1963–64 would be the use of color film. Although CBS would continue to telecast the series in black and white, Desilu felt that color productions would command higher residuals when sold as reruns.

"The Lucy Show" launched its second season with a particularly colorful episode, "Lucy Plays Cleopatra," a spoof of the then current movie epic starring Elizabeth Taylor. Equally grand was "Kiddie Parties, Inc.," an episode that ended with Lucy being lifted into the air and offstage clinging to a cluster of helium-filled balloons.

In spring 1964, Lucy welcomed back writer-producer Jess Oppenheimer for a "Lucille Ball Comedy Hour" special, based on Sherwood Schwartz's play, *Mr. and Mrs.* Bob Hope guest-starred in the play-within-a-play about a woman studio boss who wants Hope to star in a TV show about an ideal married couple.

By the end of "The Lucy Show"'s second season, Vivian Vance had grown weary of commuting and wanted to spend more time at her home in Connecticut. When Madelyn Pugh Martin announced that she was planning to remarry and leave the show, Lucy decided it was indeed time to call it quits. CBS, however, wanted another season of the top-rated comedy (according to Nielsen, it was the sixth most popular show of the season), and with Desilu still faltering as a company, Lucy capitulated. Viv promised to return the following fall only if she would not be expected to appear in every episode. And with the departure of Bob and Madelyn, a pool of new writers was assembled to pen the weekly scripts.

Garry Moore's daily radio program came to an end during the

A. Which way to the fire?
B. Vivian's acrophobia puts Lucy's attempts to save money on vertical hold when the girls decide to put up their own antenna.

183

summer of 1964, and CBS asked Lucy to replace him. Her program would be called "Let's Talk to Lucy" and consist of daily ten-minute discussions with celebrity guests.

August 31, 1964—a Monday, of course—was "Lucy Day" at the New York World's Fair where the redhead was guest of honor at the gala international tribute, which included festivities at a dozen pavillions. By 1964, "I Love Lucy" and "The Lucy Show" were visible in forty-four countries around the world, dubbed in seven different languages. As part of the eleven-hour tribute, a special film was prepared comprising "Lucy" performances dubbed in Japanese, French, Spanish, and German.

"The Lucy Show" glided into its third season with Mrs. Carmichael attending a country club dance in a pair of too-tight-to-come-off rollerskates. The next week marked Vivian's first night off, and Jack Benny guested as a frustrated plumber. (Bob Hope also made a brief appearance as Jack's assistant.)

Later that autumn, "The Lucy Show" presented an episode entitled "Lucy Becomes a Father." (Well, why not? During the past sixteen years, the zany comedienne had defied every other law of nature.) The story line concerned a father-and-son camping trip, and Lucy, not wanting her son to miss out, volunteered herself as a substitute for her late husband. The program included a marvelous scene in which Lucy gets caught in a sleeping bag and another in which the blustering Mr. Mooney comes face to face with a wild bear.

Vivian was off the night of December 28, and in her absence, Lucy's guest was Danny Kaye. In a scene reminiscent of the one staged ten years earlier with William Holden, Lucy managed to spill a tray of food in the lap of the bewildered song-and-dance man.

A new character was added to the show in February when Ann Sothern made four appearances as the beautiful but penniless Countess Framboise (alias Rosie Harrigan), an old school chum.

The "Lucy" company outdid themselves for "Lucy Meets Arthur Godfrey," with Lucy and Viv staging an old-fashioned riverboat revue for charity. A full score of original songs was written especially for Desilu by actor Max Showalter.

Although CBS renewed "The Lucy Show" for the 1965–66 season and promised to begin tele-casting it in color, Vivian Vance elected not to return for a fourth year. Accordingly, an all-new format was developed, with Lucy Carmichael and banker Mooney both moving to sunny California. (Lucy's children were sent away to boarding schools, and would not be seen.)

This new "Lucy Show" premiered with "Lucy Visits Marineland," a produced-on-location segment featuring baseball's Jimmy Piersall. Also in the cast were Harvey Korman, Lucie Arnaz, fourteen, and Desi Arnaz, Jr., twelve. This first program established the characters in their new locale, packed off Lucy's son to a military academy, and concluded with a classic scene: Lucy emerging from a pool with a playful porpoise.

The following week, Mary Jane Croft joined the series as next-door

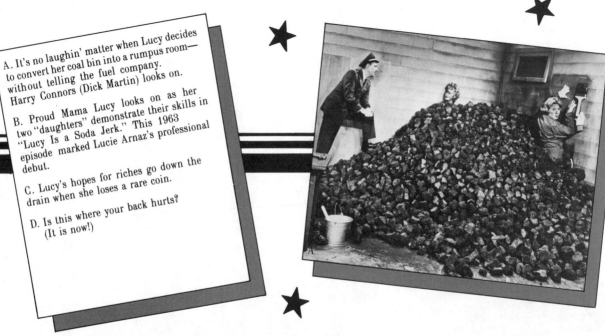

A. It's no laughin' matter when Lucy decides to convert her coal bin into a rumpus room—without telling the fuel company. Harry Connors (Dick Martin) looks on.

B. Proud Mama Lucy looks on as her two "daughters" demonstrate their skills in "Lucy Is a Soda Jerk." This 1963 episode marked Lucie Arnaz's professional debut.

C. Lucy's hopes for riches go down the drain when she loses a rare coin.

D. Is this where your back hurts? (It is now!)

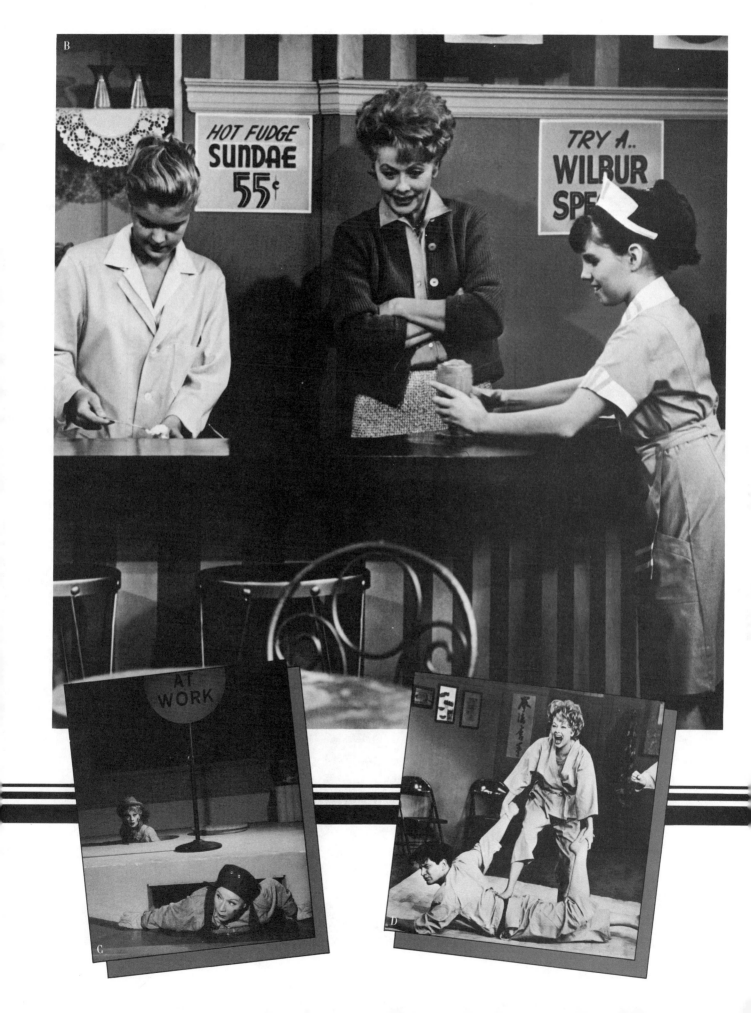

A

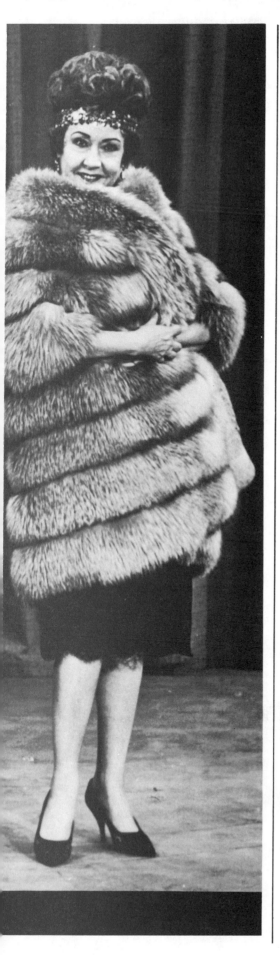

neighbor Mary Jane Lewis (her real-life married name). She would, in essence, be replacing Vivian as Lucy's official conspirator. Other tenants in Lucy's new apartment building "closely resembled" Joan Blondell, Keith Andes, and Mel Torme, each of whom guest-starred in early-season episodes.

On October 25, Lucy was reunited with two old pals: Ann Sothern and William Frawley. Bill, on camera for less than a minute, did a walk-on as a stable master. It was his last performance with his favorite redhead—he died five months later, on March 3, 1966, of a heart attack.

In the "Lucy Helps Danny Thomas" episode of November 1, Lucy Carmichael officially became banker Mooney's new secretary, with this and subsequent scripts being built around their employee-employer relationship. The bulk of the weekly plots, however, would soon be dependent upon the unsuspecting guest stars who week after week wandered into Lucy's life.

On February 14, 1966—Valentine's Day—the unsuspecting guest turned out to be Dean Martin in an episode that Miss Ball considered her personal favorite for that season. In the story, Lucy makes a blind date with Martin's look-alike stuntman. He has to work late, so Dean substitutes as Lucy's escort—but neglects to tell Lucy of the switch.

"Lucy Meets George Burns" launched the fifth year of "The Lucy Show" in the fall of 1966. Mrs. Carmichael teamed up with the cigar waver for a riotous nightclub routine reminiscent of the great "Burns and Allen" act. Carol Burnett joined Lucy for a two-part program later that fall, playing a shy librarian, and Jim Nabors, John Wayne, Phil Silvers, Hal

Lucy's right-hand man, hubby Gary Morton, guest-starred as her golfer boyfriend.

Gale Gordon got a new slant on life after joining "The Lucy Show" in 1963.

A. The Redhead Meets the Merm in a two-part episode reuniting the two actresses for the first time since *Kid Millions*, 1934.

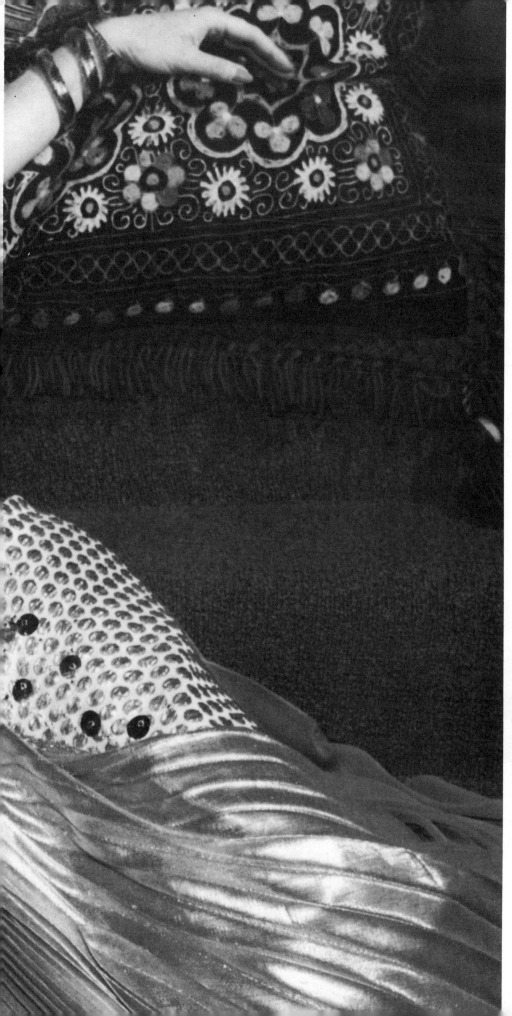

March, and Milton Berle also stopped by for visits with the wacky redhead.

On October 24, CBS telecast "Lucy in London," a one-hour special filmed in England, in which Lucy received an unorthodox—but colorful—introduction to the British capital by tour guide Anthony Newley.

On Sunday evening, June 4, 1967, the National Academy of Television Arts and Sciences presented Lucille Ball with an Emmy in recognition of her work that season in "The Lucy Show." She accepted the statuette with the remark: "The last time I got one of these, I thought they gave it to me because I'd had a baby," and then she started to cry. "That baby's fourteen years old now. I love my work; thank you for giving me this for it."

"The Lucy Show" continued to top the weekly rating charts throughout the 1967–68 season. Among the personalities appearing that year were Jacques Bergerac, Frankie Avalon, Jack Benny, Robert Goulet, Dennis

Queen of the Nile.

It's molting season when the cub scouts spend the night in Lucy's living room.

Sorry, wrong number!

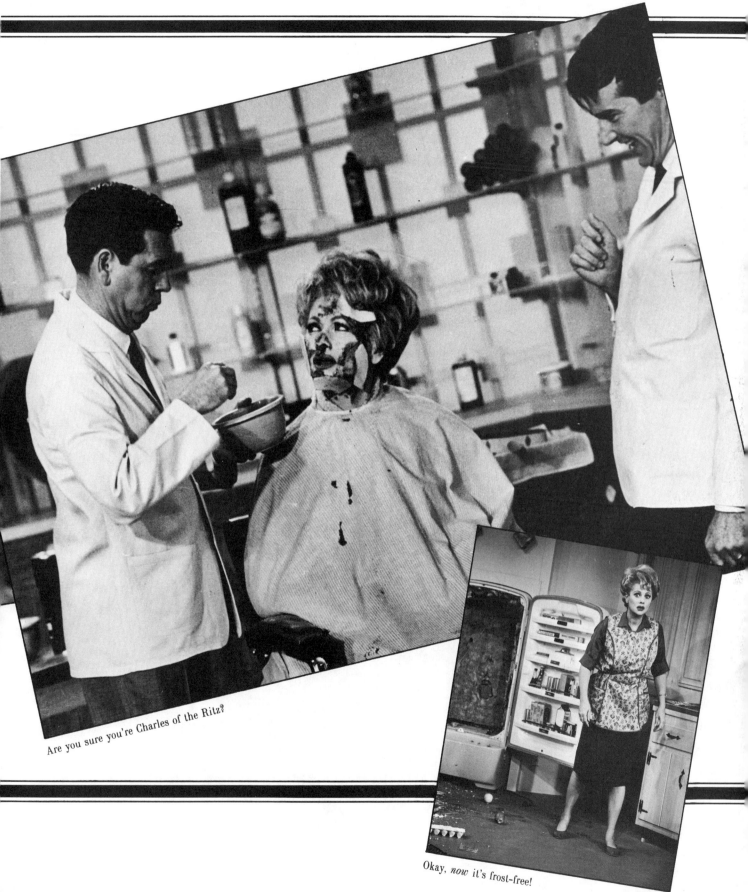

Are you sure you're Charles of the Ritz?

Okay, *now* it's frost-free!

Lu

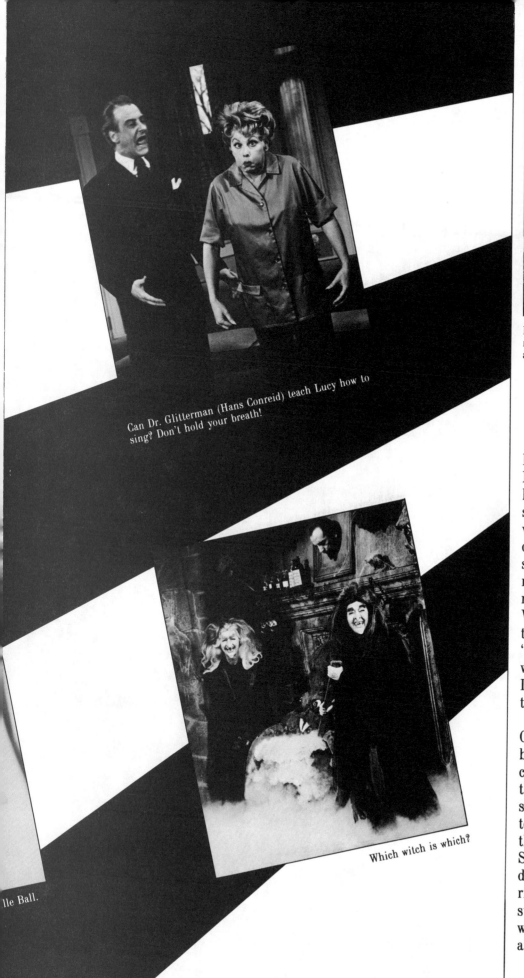

Can Dr. Glitterman (Hans Conreid) teach Lucy how to sing? Don't hold your breath!

Which witch is which?

...lle Ball.

Betty Furness, who once did refrigerator commercials on "Desilu Playhouse," stopped in for a visit on "Let's Talk to Lucy."

Day, and Carol Burnett. For the New Year's Day show, former regular Vivian Vance was the guest star, with much of the episode devoted to nostalgic flashbacks drawn from "Lucy" segments first shown in 1962–63. Joan Crawford made a rare TV appearance in a musical episode that also featured Vivian, and on March 11, Lucy tried to help Mr. Mooney win a "Boss of the Year" citation. This was the 156th segment of "The Lucy Show" and was destined to be the last.

By then, Desilu's merger with Gulf and Western Industries had become effective, and Lucy began considering her future. She knew that she wanted to continue to be self-employed and that she wanted to work in weekly television. Now that G & W owned "The Lucy Show," she asked her writers to dream up yet *another* "Lucy" series format. Did she have any suggestions? Yes—two. She wanted her own youngsters, Lucie and Desi, Jr., to co-star.

Our "Fair" Lady—Lucy receives a silver medallion from James K. Kealoka, representing the state of Hawaii, during "Lucy Day" festivities at the New York World's Fair.

A. Lucy discovers that hired help isn't what it used to be.

B. Lucy decides to redecorate. Oh, no!

C. Professor Henry Higgins would have been proud when the Countess Framboise opened a charm school and transformed charwoman Lucy into a society matron.

A

B

C

Lucy and Viv scout new talent for the Danfield Community Players.

Desi Arnaz and others consider Lucy to be the greatest master of comedy since Chaplin.

Even without Viv, Lucy and Gale made beautiful music together.

Two chumps on a log: Lucy and Ann count calories at a rustic fat farm.

Lucille Ball.

Hail Britannia! Lucy gets a fish-eye view of the river Thames.

"You look like someone I used to know."

"Why didn't you tell me you're Dean Martin? I'd have gone out with you anyway."

It's a dog's life!

Lucy wins an Emmy, June 4, 1967.

200

Lucille Ball.

Once More, Here's Lucy

★★★★★

American society was in a state of flux in 1968, and not the least of the nation's problems was a serious breakdown in communication between parent and child. Politics, morality, dress codes, music, sex, drugs, and a war in faraway Asia were typical topics that stifled intrafamily conversation. The new Lucille Ball series, "Here's Lucy," attempted to bridge and satirize the "generation gap"—Lucy-style.

Developed by veteran comedy writers, Milt Josefsberg and Bob O'Brien, "Here's Lucy" featured the wacky redhead as Lucy Carter, a Los Angeles widow with two teenaged children, Kim (Lucie Arnaz) and Craig (Desi Arnaz, Jr.). Lucy worked as a secretary for her brother-in-law, Harrison Otis Carter (Gale Gordon), proprietor of the Unique Employment Agency. Lucy—being Lucy—became involved in more "unique" situations than Harry would have liked.

The premiere episode of September 23, 1968, found Mama Carter scheming to land her children jobs entertaining at a posh birthday party. Kim loses her voice, and at the last minute, you-know-who substitutes as the vocalist with Craig's rock 'n' roll band.

Lucille Ball.

Subsequent shows had the Carters visiting Jack Benny's home, Lucy helping Shelley Winters lose weight, Lucy and Harry buying a worthless gold mine, Lucy allowing a famous authoress to hide out at the Carter home, and Lucy coaxing Van Johnson to attend a Texas birthday party for a cow!

Unfortunately, many of these early episodes were underdeveloped and vapid. This was a result of too many stories built around elements external to the Carter family situation. Rex Reed, in reviewing the series for *Women's Wear Daily,* called the show "terrible," adding "I love Lucy, but these scripts have got to get better." Cleveland Amory, in *TV Guide,* agreed: "While we loved "I Love Lucy," we can't even make friends with this show. It's the old Lucy all right, and she does her zany darndest to make you give a damn, but the trouble is, you don't."

When the writers did create a few internal family episodes, the series sparkled. One delightful segment had Lucy mistakenly thinking Kim had eloped. Another found the kids planning a birthday surprise for Mom, and in still a third, Kim started her first part-time job.

As always, the brightest moments in these "Lucy" adventures were slapstick. In one show, Lucy has a run-in with a department store dummy and later falls down the store's trash chute into a room laden with rubbish. The segment in which Lucy believes Kim to be eloping included a Laurel and Hardy-style "reciprocal destruction" scene wherein Uncle Harry and a man at the license bureau (Jack Donohue) each patiently tear each other's garments to shreds.

On December 16, 1968, the new show merged briefly with those of the recent past via a special visit by Vivian Vance. The reunion found Lucy arranging a date for Harry through a computer-dating service—which matched him with Lucy's chum, Vivian Jones. The rest of the plot was self-sustaining, with Vivian and Harry sparring and Lucy trying to keep the two together.

"Lucy and the Great Airport Chase," an experiment in on-location production, removed the redhead from her live studio audience for the first time in seventeen years. The episode was actually a pilot for an idea Lucy had had for filming selected segments of her show in various U.S. cities. Her new company, Lucille Ball Productions, acquired a mobile-truck unit and moved out to Los Angeles International Airport to film a script that pitted supersleuth Lucy Carter against a brace of se-

Meet the Carters: Lucy, Kim, and Craig, portrayed by Lucille Ball, Lucie Arnaz, and Desi Arnaz, Jr.

cret agents. It was an amusing game of hide-and-seek, as the agents pursued Lucy and Harry around the airport. The chase included a frenzied trip down a baggage chute, up an escalator, through tunnels, down a window washer's rigging, and into refrigerators. As a story, the program fell short, but as a test film to explore the potential of location shooting, the show was a success. In February, Lucille Ball renewed her contract for the 1969–70 season, announcing that for the coming year, "Here's Lucy" would take to the road.

On April 1, 1969, Lucy engaged veteran director George Marshall to direct selected episodes of "Here's Lucy"'s second season. Marshall had worked with her in 1942 on RKO's *Valley of the Sun* and again in 1950 on Paramount's *Fancy Pants* with Bob Hope, but this would be their first television project together. Within a month, Marshall's cast and crew began production in Colorado Springs on the first of eight projected location shows.

"Lucy Goes to the Air Force Academy," the first entertainment film to use the U.S. Air Force Academy facilities, premiered Lucy's eighteenth video season. Told in two parts, it was followed by a pair of additional location shows filmed near Page, Arizona. All four programs were tied together by a story line whereby Uncle Harry agrees to drive a camper to San Francisco for a client and makes the foolish mistake of taking Lucy and the children along for the ride. Lucy relieves Harry at the wheel and, entirely on her own, decides to take a side trip to Colorado Springs.

On October 27, Lucille welcomed her first "guest star" of the season, Patty Andrews. During this delightful program, Lucy, Kim, and Patty revive the sounds and styles of the famous Andrews Sisters vocal group of the forties. Johnny Carson appeared on "Here's Lucy" December 1 and received the same treatment given William Holden in 1955 and Danny Kaye in 1964. The episode ended with Lucy inadvertently dumping a trayful of drinks all over Johnny.

Vivian Vance returned in January for her annual visit, this time staying for two successive episodes. The first found Lucy and Mary Jane Croft scheming to fulfill a promise to introduce Viv to Lawrence Welk, and the second, a trip to Tijuana, involved a customs inspection crisis at the Mexican border.

The 1969–70 "Here's Lucy" product was substantially better than that of the first season. Lucy, Gale, and the Arnaz children worked together more as a team, and the scripts were finally being built around authentic family

problems—buying a second car for the children, letting them adopt a dog, making the kids earn their own money, etc. Mama Lucy was also no longer the only laugh-getter. Gale Gordon's role was evolving away from the bombastic straight man of earlier years into a well-rounded character. In one show, Lucie Arnaz was given the opportunity to dress up and impersonate an uninhibited Brooklyn secretary—with accent to match. When Unique Employment Agency came out "Eunuch," poor Harry almost had heart failure.

On February 16, the fifth and final "location" show of the season was broadcast and found the Carters visiting Las Vegas and working on singer Wayne Newton's nearby ranch. Three remaining location shows had been planned but were canceled when production costs proved excessive. The series, however, had been renewed for 1970–71, and for a time Lucy hoped to shoot episodes in Hawaii, Alaska, and Florida. These, too, were shelved when a more exciting—and expensive—situation presented itself: globetrotting superstars Richard Burton and Elizabeth Taylor virtually volunteered to appear in the first episode of the new season.

By the time Burton told Ball that he was interested in appear-ing on her show, all sixteen of "Here's Lucy"'s contributing writers were busy on other scripts, none of which could be quickly reworked to accommodate the casting of the Burtons. It was then that loyalty and old associations paid off: Lucy put in an emergency call to Bob Carroll and Madelyn Pugh Martin, now Madelyn Davis, who had not penned a "Lucy" story in over six years. Drawing on a "stunt" originally used for "I Love Lucy" in 1952, the pair whipped together a script, "Lucy Meets the Burtons," in little over a week, and the show was readied for immediate production.

In the story line, a harassed Richard Burton dresses as a plumber to escape his admiring fans and is promptly pressed into service by Lucy, who needs a faucet repaired. Before long, Burton is reciting Shakespeare in the washroom and Lucy has Liz's sixty-nine-carat ring stuck on her finger. Complicating matters, Liz and the ring are to be presented to the Hollywood press corps within a few hours. Lucy ultimately saves the day when she suggests that Miss Taylor stand in front of a curtain while meeting the press, with Lucy herself positioned immediately behind her, out of view. Liz hides her own right arm inside a free-flowing gown, substituting Lucy's diamond-clad arm, which is thrust through from behind the drape.

The stunt, a reworking of a sight gag used on both "I Love Lucy" and "The Lucy Show," wowed the audience. When the ratings were tabulated, *Here's Lucy* was listed as the number one program of the fall premiere week, racking up 52 percent of the audience and the second largest "Lucy" rating in history. This would rate as "Here's Lucy"'s finest hour . . . er, half hour. Never again would so many Americans be clustered around their television sets at one time to watch Lucy in action. More importantly, "Lucy Meets the Burtons" reunited Lucy with Bob and Madelyn, who would continue to contribute scripts to each of the series' remaining seasons.

Lucy's portfolio of programs for 1970–71 was as varied as any package ever produced for a "Lucy" season. One episode found Lucy Carter skydiving, while another pitted her against a manufacturer's consumer affairs department. Both Sammy Davis, Jr., and Buddy Rich visited the series, the Rich segment including excellent footage of Buddy and Desi, Jr. on the drums.

The days of the college musicals were revived for the program of October 19, in which Uncle Harry was staging a college alumni show for his class reunion. The program included such tunes as "Buckle Down Winsocki," from Lucy's MGM musical, *Best Foot Forward*.

One of the best programs of the season was titled "Lucy and Jack Benny's Biography," in which Jack hires Lucy to be his secretary while he dictates his life story. As

A. Trying to be as inconspicuous as possible . . .

B. There oughta be a law! Only Lucy could start out to help her son get his driver's license and wind up with a traffic ticket. Jack Gilford (left) co-starred as the harried driving inspector.

he reminisces, his past comes to life—with Lucy portraying all the women who guided his career.

For the first time in seventeen years, Lucy was pregnant again—this time disguised by a pillow—in a hilarious episode in which Lucy poses as Harry's expectant wife. Another episode found Harry becoming the new Sheridan Whiteside, when he comes to dinner at the Carter homestead—and stays, and stays, and stays.

Desi Arnaz, Jr., retired from "Here's Lucy" at the conclusion of the 1970–71 season to pursue other acting interests. In another change, the series moved production sites from its longtime home at Desilu/Paramount to Universal City Studios.

To launch the fourth season of "Here's Lucy," Bob and Madelyn created an episode guest-starring TV's most popular new comedian, Flip Wilson. Titled "Lucy and Flip Go Legit," it concluded with an inspired show-within-a-show, a satirical takeoff on *Gone With the*

Wind. After thirty-three years, Lucille was getting her chance to play Katy Scarlett O'Hara, belle of the Old South. Gale Gordon portrayed the dashing Rhett Butler, and Lucie was a very pregnant Mellie. The spotlight, of course, was on Flip, who was featured in drag as a liberated, jive-talking Prissy.

Guest stars, as always, played an important part in the 1971–72 shows, with Tony Randall, Kaye Ballard, Dinah Shore, Rich Little, Allan Funt, and Gary Morton all making early-season appearances.

Ginger Rogers, Lucy's mentor at RKO back in the thirties, came out of semiretirement for the "Here's Lucy" segment of November 8. Filmed in early summer, the episode was a testimony to the "Lucy" company's true professionalism. Facing an impending actors' strike, the cast and crew rehearsed and filmed "Ginger Rogers Comes to Tea" in only one day, instead of the usual four. Included were bits of nostalgia about Miss Rogers' old

With Lucy around, there was always "danger," as comedian Sid Gould could testify. Sid—Gary Morton's cousin—appeared in nearly every episode of "Here's Lucy" as the poor schnook who had the misfortune of crossing Lucy's path.

Little Big Mouth: Lucy Carter, vacationing in Arizona, unwittingly becomes the bride of an Indian chief.

Johnny-Come-Lucy: The redhead stumps the Carson show band (with an obscure ditty called "Snoops the Lawyer") and wins a free dinner with Johnny. His wardrobe may never be the same.

2001: A Space Lunacy.

Boogie Woogie Bugle Girls—Lucy, Patty, and Kim recreate the forties magic of Patty, Maxine, and LaVerne Andrews.

The Queen B's of Comedy.

movies and a dance routine between her, Lucy, and Lucie Arnaz.

Helen Hayes, often considered "The First Lady of the American Theatre," met "The First Lady of Television" when she guest-starred in "Lucy and the Little Old Lady." Miss Hayes appeared as a superstitious Irish dowager whom Harry suspects has swindled him out of $5,000. The Carters arrange a seance, pretend to be Napoleon and Josephine, and with the help of the supernatural, persuade the lady to return the money. The never-satisfied Harry then discovers that had he not been so hasty, his investment would have soon doubled in value.

"Lucy's Punctured Romance" teamed Lucille Ball with Bob Cummings. The twosome strike up a romance, but Kim fears that he is a philanderer and sets out with Uncle Harry to derail the budding affair.

"With Viv as a Friend, Who Needs an Enemy?" would be Vivian Vance's farewell visit to "Here's Lucy." For the show, Bob and Madelyn came up with a wonderful script in which Lucy and Harry fight, she resigns, and Harry hires Lucy's visiting pal Vivian as a replacement.

"Kim Moves Out" was another "Here's Lucy" masterpiece. Also a Carroll-Davis creation, this story was built solidly on a situation readily identifiable by all of the audience: Kim wants to move into her own apartment; Mama Lucy doesn't want to see her "baby" leave. It was a classic, but also a prelude to the final episode of the season, a spin-off pilot for a new "Lucie Arnaz Show," entitled "Kim Finally Cuts You-Know-Who's Apron Strings."

CBS did not buy the proposed new series, but by January 1972, it didn't matter, because Lucy had suddenly broken her leg while skiing in Colorado, and Lucie would be needed now more than ever to maintain "Here's Lucy." Doctors had warned that Lucy would have to wear some sort of cast during the production of all twenty-four episodes for 1972–73, so the writers planned no strenuous activities for the redhead.

"Lucy's Big Break" opened "Here's Lucy"'s fifth season with the bewildered Lucy lying in a hospital bed, her leg in traction. Bob and Madelyn wove this premiere story around the plight of the lonely invalid—who, before long, falls madly in love with her attending physician.

Five subsequent programs revolved around the broken-leg situation, with Lucy first in the hospital, then recuperating at home, and finally getting around in a motorized wheelchair.

Desi, Jr., returned to his mother's side that season for "Lucy and Joe Namath," in which a frustrated Craig Carter turns to the New York Jets quarterback for advice on how to overcome his own

More lemons than a fruit stand. Lucy tries to outsmart the shyster used-car dealer (Milton Berle) who sold her children a clunker.

Ring-a-Ding-Ding! Dingaling Lucy does it again when she gets Elizabeth Taylor's $1.5 million diamond ring stuck on her finger.

mother's objections to football. Petula Clark, Donny Osmond, and Jim Bailey guest-starred in subsequent shows.

"Lucy and Harry's Pot" was a touching story in which Lucy accidentally fractures a piece of treasured pottery that was made for Harry by a previous secretary. When a fast repair job seems impossible, Lucy enrolls herself in an art class and turns out something less than a ceramic masterpiece.

Says Lucy tenderly, "Harry, I know she made a better-looking vase than I did . . . but that doesn't mean she liked you any better." Such open affection had not been expressed in a "Lucy" production since the Ricardos hugged the Mertzes.

In the spring of 1972, Lucille Ball had signed with Warner Bros. to star in their motion picture version of the musical *Mame*. No one, including Lucy, knew whether,

after finishing the picture, she would want to attempt a sixth season of "Here's Lucy." To cover themselves, the TV company fashioned "Lucy and Harry's Memoirs," a retrospective episode to air as the final program of the 1972–73 season. In the premise, Harry has sold the family business, and he and Lucy reminisce about their many misadventures together. In the last scene, Lucy scrawls the word "temporarily" on

their "Out of Business" sign, then winks directly at the camera before exiting. This somewhat ambiguous ending allowed the writers room for invention—just in case there should be a 1973-74 season.

It did not take the redhead long to decide. In January 1973, with *Mame* going before the cameras, Lucy announced that, yes, she would return to CBS in the fall. Unfortunately, the decision had been made more with her heart

than with her head, for clearly "Here's Lucy" was running out of good ideas.

Of the twenty-four programs produced for "Here's Lucy"'s sixth season (Lucy's twenty-third year on TV), only a few seemed charming or original. "Lucy Is N. G. As R. N." was a refreshing throwback to the old days, with Lucy going it alone—with no guest stars. She dons a nurse's cap to care for a houseful of invalids—

Harry, who has a sprained knee; Kim, who is bedridden with a cold; Mary Jane, who has broken a finger on each hand; and Kim's cat—also named Harry—who is very, very pregnant.

"Lucy Meets Lucille Ball" was the ultimate spoof of the Lucy-meets-a-celebrity routine. Filmed in pieces and spliced together, this very clever show featured Lucy as "Lucille Ball, Hollywood Star" and "Lucy Carter, Housewife," in-

Lucy and Kim give it that
"old college try" when they
accompany Harry to a class
reunion.

volved in—what else?—a Lucille
Ball look-alike contest.

"Lucy Fights the System," the
144th and final "Here's Lucy"
production, was something of an
allegorical statement about modern society. When a competent, experienced waitress is fired—simply because she is no longer young
—Lucy sets out to teach the
youth-oriented employer a lesson.
She arranges to have Kim hired as
the waitress's flashy replacement,

and Kim, in a tour de force performance, proceeds to turn the restaurant into a shambles. Desper-
ate, the man is all too happy to hire
his old reliable waitress back.

The final laugh of the evening,
however, belonged to Gale Gordon,
who managed to catch one last pie
in the face. Wiping the whipped
cream from his brow, the exas-
perated comedian looked directly
into the camera and sighed: "I
knew it would end like this."

Love is no longer in bloom, as Jack Benny tells his movie-star girl friend that their romance is over.

Desi, Jr., once part of the Dino, Desi, and Billy singing group, joined Ann-Margret in a musical episode.

Approaching Yankees and birthing babies were small problems for Scarlett compared with the sarcasm supplied by this Prissy.

Someone's on the ski lift with Dinah, and it wasn't Jean Claude Killy.

It's Good Night Nurse . . .
when Harry is enlisted to care for the vol

Love that Bob!

Seems like old times . . .

Lucy
the C
worst

The Green-Eyed Monster gets the best of guest
Totie Fields, who thinks her milkman husband
is being too attentive to the recuperating Lucy.

"The Unemployment Follies" teamed Lucy and Carol Burnett in a takeoff on "The Dolly
Sisters."

Two lor
scored l
"The Bi

e invalid.

Lucy learns the bear facts about mountain climbing.

ABSOLUTELY NO SMOKING

KDEX COLOR

d Kim were really in a pickle when
rs appeared in a commercial for the
ing product since Vitameatavegamin.

UNIVERSITY OF SOUTHERN CALIFORNIA

tance runners, Lucy and O. J.,
galore when they teamed up for
e" episode.

"Dirty Gertie" Lucy helps police infiltrate a gang of mobsters, borrowing a
page from Damon Runyon's "Apple Annie" character.

217

Lucille Ball.

Forever, Lucy

After a quarter century of madcap antics, Lucille Ball experimented with light drama.

*L*ucille Ball was faced with a dilemma throughout the twenty-three-year run of her various "Lucy" series. Did the American public love *her*—Lucille Ball, the actress—or did they love "Lucy"—the scatterbrained redhead—or did they love both? Would they accept her—Lucille—in other roles? How far from the "Lucy" character would she be allowed to stray?

The question was put to the test with the motion picture *Mame.* In discussing the final script, Miss Ball told the press, "We tried to keep most of the Lucy character out. There are a couple of slapstick moments that I'm sure people will associate with 'Lucy' . . . but we avoided that as much as possible and put in what was always supposed to be there from the 'Auntie Mame' script."

Although production was delayed almost a year because of Lucy's broken leg, *Mame* went before the cameras in January 1973, with Gene Saks directing. Saks's wife, Bea Arthur, Robert Preston, Jane Connell, Bruce Davison, and Kirby Furlong completed the cast.

Mame would be the fifth retelling of the story created by Patrick Dennis in 1954 about a life-loving, freewheeling grande dame aunt who must raise her orphaned

219

She coaxed the blues right out of the horn . . .

nephew. The story was originally created for a novel, then adapted as a Broadway play, then adapted for a movie version of the play, then rewritten into a Broadway musical. Lucy, starring in the motion picture of that musical, would be following in the footsteps of Rosalind Russell and Angela Lansbury, both of whom had played "Auntie Mame" triumphantly in earlier versions.

The picture was in production for nearly six months and in post-production a similar length of time. It had its "world premiere" at a special showing at Lincoln Center for the Performing Arts on February 25, 1974, then moved to Radio City Music Hall to play as the Easter presentation.

Never before had the critical response to a Lucille Ball movie been so passionate and yet so di-

vided. *Variety* loved it, saying *"Mame* is why movies were invented," but Judith Crist, in *New York* magazine, referred to it as "Auntie Maimed." Composer Jerry Herman thought it did great justice to his music, called it "a whammy of a show," but Pauline Kael found it a "hippopotamic musical." And although *After Dark* magazine presented Lucy with its annual Ruby Award as

A. Mame Dennis, Three Beekman Place, New York City. B. Her best beau—Beauregard Jackson Pickett Burnside.

"Entertainer of the Year," *Films in Review* lamented, "She does not possess that larger-than-life movie star quality which this musical needs."

Despite the critical controversy, *Mame* did exceptionally well at Radio City, and, thanks to a nationwide personal appearance tour by Lucille Ball, it continued to do well throughout the country.

Lucy returned to television dur-ing the 1974–75 season with two hour-long comedy specials on CBS. The first, "Happy Anniversary and Goodbye," teamed her with Art Carney, as a couple who decide to separate after twenty-five years of marriage.

"Lucy Gets Lucky," a brand-new "Lucy" adventure, took the redhead to Las Vegas where she had plans to see Dean Martin's nightclub show. Physical hijinks were the order of the day, with men falling off ladders, Lucy botching a series of odd jobs in a Las Vegas casino, then being chased through the MGM Grand Hotel by men she believes to be gangsters.

Planning two more specials for 1975–76, Lucy decided to attempt material that was totally different from anything she had ever done for television. Both of the shows consisted of three interrelated

Mame and Vera: friends, sisters, and pals . . .

comedy sketches, the first program teaming her with Jackie Gleason, the second with Art Carney once again.

The Gleason hour, titled "Three for Two," was based on material written by Renee Taylor and Joseph Bologna, and directed by Charles Walters. Unfortunately, it marked the low point in both Lucy's and Gleason's television careers. *Variety*, historically in Lucy's corner, called it "a dismal trio of one-act plays about unpleasant and stupid people."

"What Now, Catherine Curtis?," co-starring Carney, fared much better. A trilogy of short plays related the comic experiences and emotional readjustment of a divorcée in her middle years. The first playlet was a monologue, with Catherine, newly divorced after more than twenty years of marriage, moving into her own new apartment. Carney appeared in act two as a carpenter to whom Catherine takes a shine, and Joseph Bologna co-starred in act three as the younger man with whom Catherine falls in love.

The year 1976 marked not only the bicentennial of the United States, but also Lucille Ball's twenty-fifth anniversary with CBS Television. To mark the event, the network and Lucy's production

company came up with a humdinger of a special, two hours' worth of *CBS Salutes Lucy: The First 25 Years*, featuring film clips and on-camera testimonials by every major star who had worked with the redhead over the years. Highlights included appearances by Desi, Sr., Vivian Vance, and Gale Gordon, and, of course, the vintage "Lucy" clips.

A second "reunion" special was planned in 1977, this time a brand-new "Lucy" production that would reteam her with Vivian, Gale, Mary Jane Croft, and Mary Wickes. Bob Carroll and Madelyn Davis wrote and co-produced the outing, which found midwestern Lucy Whittaker preparing to meet

Norma and Malcolm Michaels discover that their marriage—and their waistlines—aren't what they used to be.

the President, Jimmy Carter.

"Lucy Calls the President" was destined to be the last major "Lucy" production for CBS Television. In 1978, Lucille Ball "guest-hostessed" a country-western variety hour for the network, but in the summer of 1979, she suddenly switched allegiance and signed a contract with NBC. Among the reasons for the change was NBC's willingness to allow Lucy to create new comedy programs starring others. She would continue to do occasional specials but had no plans for a new series to star herself. "I wouldn't mind the routine of a series," she explained, "but I'm too old to keep on being yelled

A new Lucy—"Lucy Collins"—hits the jackpot when she meets Dino in a casino.

at by Uncle Harry."

The death of Vivian Vance in August 1979 added to Lucille's reluctance to continue the "Lucy" characterizations. Indeed, when she unveiled her first NBC project, "Lucy Moves to NBC," it was clear that she would be portraying a fictionalized version of herself, Lucille Ball, the actress-producer, not "Lucy," the scatterbrained redhead. The change, however subtle, was but one in a series of new images Lucy has donned over the years. As we have seen, she has been a showgirl, a starlet, a star, a model, an actress, a comedienne, a wife, and a mother. She has been both a student and a teacher in the Hollywood school of survival.

Her roles have been varied and many. For Broadway audiences Lucy will be remembered as Wildcat Jackson. For film buffs she will always be Madame DuBarry, Her Highness in *The Big Street*, and, certainly, Mame. Radio listeners fondly recall the foibles of madcap Liz Cooper. But for anyone who has ever watched Lucy Ricardo prying up footprints in front of Grauman's Chinese Theatre, or Lucy Carmichael installing her own TV antenna, or Lucy Carter riding the rapids on a rubber raft, Lucy will always be "Lucy"—and she will never be forgotten.

Gypsy in Her Soul—Lucy joined Shirley MacLaine in a salute to the ladies and gentlemen of the chorus line.

Lucille Ball.

A

B

A. Jackie Gleason not only joined Lucy on her own special in December 1975, but also on the annual Entertainer of the Year Awards. Lucy received the "Golden Award" from the American Guild of Variety Artists.

B. Lucy Opens Up: In a conversation with Barbara Walters, Lucy and Gary discussed the warmth and love that has held their marriage together.

C. Proud as a Peacock, eleven-year-old Gary Coleman led a parade of guest stars on a special welcoming of Lucy to NBC, February 8, 1980.

D. Their Last Hurrah: Lucy and Vivian Vance clowned one last time in "Lucy Calls the President."

C

D

Index

Page numbers in italics indicate photographs

Abbott, Bud, 99, 103
Abbott, George, 65, 69, 96,
"Abbott and Costello Show," 99
Addis, Jus, 114
Affairs of Annabel, The, 63, *65*
Agar, John, *126*
Akins, Claude, *159*
Albert, Eddie, 126
Allyson, June, 96, 99
Andes, Keith, 169, 187
Andrews, Patty, 203, *207*
Annabel Takes a Tour, 63, *66*
"Ann Sothern Show, The," 169
Antes, Jerry, *174*
Arden, Eve, 62, 63, 116, 136
Arnaz, Desi, 69, 71–72, 77, *77, 78, 80, 84–85,* 96, 98, *100,* 103, 108, *108,* 109, 112, 114, *115, 120,* 126, *126,* 127, *128,* 129, *129,* 130, *130,* 131, 132, *132,* 133, 137, *137,* 138, *138,* 139, 140, 141, *141, 142,* 145, *146, 147, 149, 151–154, 158, 159, 162,* 163, 165, *165,* 166, *166, 167, 167,* 168, 169, *170, 172, 173, 173, 174,* 175, 179, *196,* 222
Arnaz, Desi, IV, 133, 138, *152,* 163, 184, 193, 201, 203, *203,* 204, 205, 208, *214,*
Arnaz, Lucie Desiree, 131, *131,* 138, *152, 153,* 184, *185,* 193, 201, 203, *203,* 204, 205, *207,* 208, *212, 217*
Arthur, Bea, 219, *222*
Arzner, Dorothy, 68
Astaire, Fred, 44, 47, *53,* 99, *104*
Auntie Mame, 219
Averback, Hy, 119
Baker, Phil, 63, *63*
Ball, Desiree Hunt (DeDe), 14, 17, 18
Ball, Fred, 15, 112
Ball, Henry Dunnell, 14
Ball, Pamela, *115*
Bankhead, Tallulah, 12, 141
Barrie, Wendy, *71*
Bataan, 98, *100,* 109
Beauty for the Asking, 67, *71*
Benedaret, Bea, 119
Benny, Jack, 120–121, *177,* 184, 189, *195,* 202, 204–205, *213*
Bergen, Edgar, 72, *86*
Berkeley, Busby, 41
Berle, Milton, 116, 126, 168, 169, 189, *209*
Berman, Pandro S., 47, 61, 163
Best Foot Forward, 96–98, *98,* 103, 204
Big Street, The, 72–77, 82, 83, 84, 222
Blake, Madge, 165
Blane, Ralph, 96
Bliss, Lela, *118–119*
Blondell, Joan, *73,* 187
Blood Money, 43
"Bob Hope Show, The," 114

Born Yesterday, 126
Bosley, Tom, 175
Bottoms Up, 41
Bowman, Lee, 62, *100,* 118
Bracken, Eddie, 69, *77*
Bremer, Lucille, 99
Brent, George, *111,* 112
Brice, Fanny, 100
Broadway Bill, 44
Broadway Thru a Keyhole, 43
Bunker Bean, 54
Burnett, Carol, 187, 193, *208, 216*
"Burns 'n' Allen Show," 99
Burton, Richard, 12, 204, *210*
Buzzell, Eddie, 96, 103
Cabot, Bruce, 121
Calhern, Louis, 166, *170*
Cantor, Eddie, 29, *40,* 41, 43, *43,* 114, *126*
Carlson, Richard, 69, *77*
Carnegie, Hattie, 29, 41
Carney, Art, 175, *177, 219,* 221, 222, *222*
Carnival, 44
Carroll, Bob, Jr., 119, 126, 129, 130, 131, 136, 138, 168, 173, 179, 183, 204, 205, 208, 222
Carson, Jack, 99, 114
Carson, Johnny, 203, *206*
Carter, President Jimmy, 222
"CBS Salutes Lucy: The First 25 Years," 222
Charley's Aunt, 17
Chevalier, Maurice, 114
Clark, Petula, 210
Cleveland, George, 82
Coburn, Charles, 114
Cohn, Harry, 127
Coleman, Cy, 170
Coleman, Gary, *223*
Collins, Ray, *88*
Connell, Jane, 219
Conreid, Hans, 82, *138, 193*
Cook, Elisha, Jr., *109*
Cormack, Bartlett, 49, *54*
Costello, Lou, 99, 103, *109*
Craig, James, 72, *87, 88*
Critic's Choice, 173–175, *176*
Croft, Mary Jane, 140, 182, 184–187, 203, 222
Cummings, Bob, 208, *216*
Dance, Girl, Dance, 68–69, 71, 72, *76*
"Danny Thomas Show, The," 169
Dark Corner, The, 111–112, *113*
Davenport, Bill, 116, 119
Davis, Madelyn (See: Pugh, Madelyn)
Day, Dennis, 189–193
DeMille, Cecil B., 127
Denning, Richard, 119, *122–123*

"Desilu Playhouse," 168, *193*
Desilu Workshop, *174*
Dix, Richard, 44, 67, 68, *70*
Dix, Tommy, 96, *98*

Donohue, Jack, 95–96, 103–108, 179, 203
Don't Tell the Wife, 55
Dream Girl, 114, *118,* 119, *119*
DuBarry Was a Lady, 84, 93, 94, *94,* 95, 96, 99, 131
Dunne, Irene, 44, 62
Dwan, Allan, 72
Easy Living, 118, *120,* 121, *121–122*
Easy to Wed, 103, *108,* 112
"Eddie Cantor Show, The," 114
"Ed Sullivan Show, The," 176
Ellison, James, 67
Erroll, Leon, 44, 49
Facts of Life, The, 169, 170, *174,* 175
Fancy Pants, 121, *124,* 126, 203
Father of the Bride, 165, 166
Felton, Verna, *140*
Ferber, Edna, 55
Fields, Totie, *216*
Five Came Back, 67, 71
Follow the Fleet, 47, *49, 51,* 53
Fonda, Henry, 47, 72, 83, *88,* 170, 175, 176, *177*
Ford, "Tennessee" Ernie, 133, 136, *145, 146*
Forever, Darling, 137, 166–167, *170*
Foster, Preston, *109*
Fox, Frank, 116, 119
Frank, Melvin, 169, *175*
Frawley, William, 100, 130, *135, 138, 141, 145, 146, 154, 159, 187, 198*
Freed, Arthur, 83–84, 94–95, 96, 99, 100, 103
Freund, Karl, 96, 131, *131*
Fugitive Lady, 44
Fuller Brush Girl, The, 121–126, *126*
Fuller Brush Man, The, 119
Furness, Betty, 193
Garnett, Tay, 98, *100*
Garrett, Jimmy, 179, *181*
"Garry Moore Show, The," *175*
Gaxton, William, *98*
Gilbert, Billy, *88*
Gilford, Jack, *205*
Girl, A Guy, and A Gob, A, 70–71, *79*
Gleason, Jackie, 222, *224*
Go Chase Yourself, 63
Godfrey, Arthur, 116, 184, *196*
Goldwyn, Samuel, 29, 41, 43, *43,* 44, 111, 114
Gone With the Wind, 67, *68,* 205
Good Years, The, 170, 173
Gordon, Gale, 119, *135,* 182–183, *186–187, 196, 198,* 201, 203, 204, 205, *210,* 212, *216,* 222
Gould, Sid, *206*
Grable, Betty, 47, 49, *53,* 82
Grady, Billy, 103
Granet, Bert, 65
Greatest Show on Earth, The, 127

Grey, Mack, *45*
Guide for the Married Man, A, 175, *177*
Guilaroff, Sidney, 95
Hahlo, Sylvia, 29
Hall, Alexander, 166–167
Harding, Ann, 44
Harding, Henry, 173
Hardwicke, Cedric, 72, 114
Harlow, Jean, 93, 108
Harris, Eleanor, *80*
Hart, Ralph, 179, *181*
Hartmann, Edmund, 121
Harvey, Paul, *139*
Hatch, Wilbur, *123*
Hathaway, Henry, 111
Hauser, Jerry, *139*
Haver, Ron, 59
Having Wonderful Time, 62, 63
Hays, Helen, 208
Hayward, Leland, 170
Hayward, Louis, 68, *76*
Hepburn, Katharine, 44, *59,* 60–61, 93, 96, 100
Her Husband's Affairs, 114, *118*
"Here's Lucy," 201–217, *206*
Herman, Jerry, 220
Hey Diddle Diddle, 49, *54,* 55, 115
Hilliard, Harriet, 47, *53*
Hodiak, John, 109, *109*
Holden, William, 121, 136, *147, 148,* 184, 203
Holliday, Judy, 126–127
Hope, Bob, 114, 116, *120,* 121, *124,* 139, 169, 170, 173–174, *174,* 175, *175, 176,* 183, 184, 195, 203
Horton, Edward Everett, 67, 114, *118*
Hughes, Gordon, 119, 120, *123*
Hunt, Florabelle Orchutt, 15
Hunt, Fred C., 14, 15
Hunt, Marsha, 96
Huntley, Chet, *103*
I Dream Too Much, 47
"I Love Lucy," 127, 129–159, 163, 165–169, 179, 182, 184, 202, 204
"Jack Carson Show, The," 99
Jackson, E. A. (Mrs.), 29
Jagger, Dean, 72
Jealousy, 44
Johnson, Casey, *71*
Johnson, Van, 103, 108, *108,* 175, 202
Jolson, Al, 98
Jordan, Jim, 72
Jordan, Marian, 72
Josefsberg, Milt, 201
Joy of Living, 62, *62*
Kallman, Dick, *174*
Kanin, Garson, 69
Karloff, Boris, 114
Kaye, Danny, 114, 184, 203
Kealoka, James K., *194*
Keaton, Buster, 99

Keith, Richard (See: Thibodeaux, Keith)
Kelly, Gene, 95, 96, 175
Kennedy, Harold, 114
Kern, James V., 72
Kerr, Jean, 175
Kid Millions, 42, 43, *43, 187*
Kidd, Michael, 169
King, Edith, 169
Koerner, Charles, 78, 84
"Kraft Music Hall" (radio), 99
Kyser, Kay, 67, *73*
LaCava, Gregory, 61, 62
"Lady Esther Presents Orson Welles," 98
LaGuardia, Fiorello, *73*
Lahr, Bert, 94, 95, 99, *100*
Lamont, Molly, *49*
Landis, Jessie Royce, 173
Lane, Charles, 182, 183
Lanfield, Sidney, 116
Lange, Mary, *40*
Lansbury, Angela, 100, 220
Laughton, Charles, 68, 69, 77, 121
Leeds, Andrea, 62
Leeds, Peter, 165
Leigh, Carolyn, 170
Leonard, Robert, *109*
LeRoy, Hal, 69, *77*
"Let's Talk to Lucy," *184, 193*
Levene, Sam, *88*
Lewis, Cecil Day, 69
Lewis, Elliot, 179, 182
Libeled Lady, 103, 108
Life Without George, 181
Linkletter, Art, *140*
Little, Rich, 205
Lloyd, Harold, 70
Lockhart, Gene, 114
Lombard, Carole, 68, 69, 72, 78, 116
Long, Long Trailer, The, 133, 163–166, *166,* 167
Look Who's Laughing, 72, *86*
Loper, Don, 136
Lover Come Back, 111, 112
Loy, Myrna, 108
"Lucille Ball–Desi Arnaz Show," 141, 167, 169
"Lucy Show, The," 176, 179–193, *181,* 204
Lured, 114, 115, *117,* 131
McCarthy, Charlie, 72, *86*
McKay, Scott, 114
MacLaine, Shirley, 223
MacLane, Barton, 82
Magic Carpet, The, 126, 127
Main, Marjorie, 165, *165*
Mame, 210, 211, 219–221
Manners, Dorothy, 112
Mannes, Marya, *170*
March, Hal, 119, 187–189
Marines Fly High, 67–68, *75*
Marsac, Maurice, *156*
Marshall, George, *88,* 121, 203
Martin, Dean, 187, *198, 221,* 222
Martin, Dick, 179, *184*
Martin, Hugh, 96
Martin, Madelyn Pugh (See: Pugh, Madelyn)
Martin, Quinn, 168
Marx Brothers, 65, *67,* 96
Marx, Groucho, 65

Marx, Harpo, 12, 136
Mason, James, 166, 167, *170*
Matthau, Walter, 175
Mature, Victor, 82, 83, *92,* 118
Maxwell, Marilyn, 99, 173
Meek, Donald, 95
Meet the People, 98, 99, *100, 102–103*
Menjou, Adolphe, 67
Men of the Night, 44
Merman, Ethel, 11, 43, 94, 95, *187*
Miller, Ann, *61,* 65, 69
"Milton Berle Show, The," 169
Minnelli, Liza, 166
Minnelli, Vincente, 99, 165
Miss Grant Takes Richmond, 121, *124*
Mr. and Mrs., 183
Mr. and Mrs. Smith, 69–70
Moore, Candy, 179, *181, 185*
Moore, Garry, *175,* 183
Moore, Ida, 165
Moorehead, Agnes, 82
Morgan, Frank, 96, *96*
Morris, Chester, 67, 68, *71, 72*
Morrison, Barbara, 114
Morse, Robert, 175
Morton, Gary, 170, *177, 187,* 205, *206, 223*
Mostel, Zero, 95
Mowbray, Alan, 114
Murphy, George, 43–44, 70, 71, *100*
"My Favorite Husband," 116, 118, 119, 120, 121, *122–123,* 126, 132, 167, *182–183*
Nabors, Jim, 187
Nana, 43
Namath, Joe, 208
Nash, N. Richard, 169, 170
Nasser, James, 114
Nelson, Barry, *100*
Nelson, Frank, 140, *150*
Nelson, Ozzie, 119
Newley, Anthony, 189, *198*
Newman, Bernard, *47, 48, 55*
Newton, Wayne, 204
Next Time I Marry, 65, 83
Night at the Biltmore Bowl, 47
Nolan, Lloyd, *100,* 109, 118, *120–121*
Novello, Jay, *134–135*
Nye, Louis, 169
Oakie, Jack, 63, *65*
O'Brien, Robert, 121, 201
O'Brien, Virginia, 95, 96, 99
O'Hara, Maureen, 68, 69
O'Keefe, Dennis, 67
Old Man Rhythm, 47
Olsen, Moroni, 67
One Live Ghost, 49
Oppenheimer, Jess, 100, 120, 121, 126, 129, 130, 131, 132, 136, 137, 138, 183
"Orson Welles Show, The," 99
Osmond, Donny, 210
"Our Miss Brooks," 116, 166
Paar, Jack, 118, 119
Paley, William S., 130
Pan, Hermes, 47, *56, 57*
Panama Lady, 67, *70*
Panama, Norman, 169
Panama Hattie, 94

Passage to Bordeaux, 72
Pasternak, Joseph, 96, 103
Patrick, Lee, 62
Peale, Norman Vincent, Dr., 170
Penner, Joe, 63, *63,* 67
Pepper, Barbara, *40,* 49, *55, 136*
Perfectly Mismated, 44
Petersen, Edward, 17
"Phil Baker Show, The," 63
"Philip Morris Playhouse," 99
Pierce, Hazel, *136*
Piersall, Jimmy, 184
Pommer, Erich, 68, 69, 72
Pons, Lily, 47, 49, *56*
Powell, Dick, 99, *100, 102, 103*
Powell, William, 93, 100, 108, *170*
Preston, Robert, 219, *221*
Pugh, Madelyn, 119, 126, 129, 130, 131, 136, 138, 168, 173, 179, 183, 204, 205, 208, 222
Raft, George, *45*
Randall, Tony, 205
"Reader's Digest—Radio Edition" 114
Reis, Irving, 82
Rice, Elmer, 114, *118*
Rich, Buddy, 204
Roberta, 44, 47, *47,* 112
Rogers, Charles "Buddy," 47
Rogers, Ginger, 44, 47, *53,* 55, *59–61,* 62, *62,* 63, 68, 94, 69, 205, *216*
Rogers, Lela Emogene, 44–47, *47,* 55, 62, 169
Roman Scandals, 29, *40,* 41, 43
Room Service, 65, *67,* 112
Rorick, Isabel Scott, 116
Rorke, Hayden, 114
Rose, Helen, 100
Rosten, Leo, 111, 114
Runyon, Damon, 72, 77, 78, 82, 83, 116, *217*
Saks, Gene, 219
Sanders, George, 114, *117*
Schiller, Bob, 137, 138, 179
Schwartz, Sherwood, 183
Scott, Lizabeth, 118
Scott, Randolph, 47
"Screen Guild Players," 99, 114
"Screen Guild Theatre," 98
"Sealtest Village Store," 114
Sedgewick, Edward, 99
Seiter, William A., 112
Selznick, David O., 67
Seven Days Leave, 82–83, 95, 118
Shavelson, Mel, 175
Sheekman, Arthur, 43
Shirley, Anne, 44, *48,* 49, *53,* 55
Shore, Dinah, 205, *215*
Showalter, Max, 184
Silvers, Phil, *177,* 187
Silvie, Ben, 44
Simon, S. Sylvan, 114, 119, 121, 126, 127
Simpson, O. J., *217*
Sinatra, Frank, 114
Sirk, Douglas, 114
Sisk, Robert, *75*
Skelton, Richard "Red," 63, *94,* 95, 96, 119, 120, 126, *162*
Smiler With a Knife, The, 69
So and Sew, 49, *53*
Sorrowful Jones, 120, 121, 126

Sothern, Ann, 43, 93, 95, 96, 99, 168, 169, *171,* 184, 187, *196*
Stage Door, 55, 60–62, *61,* 68
Stevens, Mark, 111, *113*
Stewart, Paula, 169
Strictly Dynamite (See: *Footlight Serenade*)
Tannen, Julius, 17
Taylor, Elizabeth, 12, 183, 204, *211*
Taylor, Kent, *71*
Tearle, Conway, 55
"Texaco Star Theatre, The," 116
That Girl From Paris, 49, *56*
That's Right, You're Wrong, 73
They Knew What They Wanted, 69
Thibodeaux, Keith, 138, *158*
Thomas, Danny, 141, 168, 187
Thorpe, Jerry, 168
Thousands Cheer, 96, *96,* 99
Three Little Pigskins, 44, *44*
Three Musketeers, The, 47
Three Stooges, The, 44, *44*
Tomkins, Dan, 169, *175*
Tone, Franchot, 114, *118*
Too Many Girls, 69–71, *77–78,* 96, 103, 109
Top Hat, 47
Tracy, Spencer, *11,* 93, 100, *106,* 108
Turner, Lana, 93, 96
Twelve Crowded Hours, 67, *70*
Twiss, Clinton, 163, 165
Two Smart People, 109, *109,* 114
Valley of the Sun, 72, *87–88,* 203
Vance, Vivian, 130, *131, 132, 134, 135, 137, 138, 141, 145–147, 150, 151, 154, 155, 157–161,* 173, 176, 179, *181, 182–184, 182–185, 193, 193, 196,* 203, *204,* 208, 222, *223*
Vigran, Herb, *144,* 165, *165*
Walker, Nancy, 96, *126*
Walters, Barbara, *224*
Walters, Charles, 95, 96, 222
Weiskopf, Bob, 137, 138, 179
Welles, Orson, 69–70, 98, 99, 139
Wickes, Mary, *133,* 182, 222
Widmark, Richard, 136
Wildcat, 169–170, *175*
Williams, Esther, 103, 108
Wilson, Flip, 205, *214–215*
Winchell, Walter, 175
Winterset, 49
Wise, Robert, *76*
Within the Law, 17
Without Love, 100, 103, *106*
Wynn, Ed, *126*
Wynn, Keenan, 100, 103, *106,* 108, *109,* 112, 165
You Can't Fool Your Wife, 68, *75*
Yours, Mine and Ours, 173, 175–176
Zanuck, Darryl F., 43
Ziegfeld, Florenz, 20, 99, *104*
Ziegfeld Follies, 99
Ziegfeld Follies of 1944/1946, 99, 100, 103, *105*
Zola, Emile, 43
Zorina, Vera, 112